An Education for the 21ˢᵗ Century

A Handbook for Teachers

Jeffrey A. Hinton

www.jeffreyahinton.com

Table of

Contents

Chapter 03 - Effective Learning for the 21st Century 71

CHAPTER

$$01$$

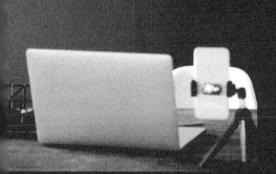

21ˢᵗ Century Skills and Why Our Students Need Them

Much education today is monumentally ineffective. All too often we are giving young people cut flowers when we should be teaching them to grow their own plants.

—JOHN W. GARDNER

In the middle of the 20th century, American public schools were considered by many to be the best in the world. Through compulsory education laws and an enormous expansion of the high-school system, students from all economic levels and backgrounds had the opportunity to attend free, taxpayer-supported public schools. This educated populous would propel the country to economic prosperity as the nation became a global economic superpower after World War II. Today, however, many stakeholders lament the American school system's condition. International test scores place America's students somewhere in the middle of tested first-world nations. In trying to determine what went wrong in American education policy, former secretary of education Arne Duncan pointed out that "About 100 years ago, America made secondary education in high school compulsory. That was almost unprecedented, a massive leap forward, and it drove a lot of our economic boom over the past 100 years. The problem is we haven't moved past that, and we haven't adjusted the model. The world is radically different from that time, but unfortunately, education isn't much different." Therein lies the crux of the problem. It is not that our schools are broken. They are working just as they were designed for a world that looked much different than it does today. The problem is that they have not evolved to meet the changing demands of an interconnected world. As Tony Wagner points out in his book *The Global Achievement Gap: Why Our Best Schools Don't Teach the New Survival Skills Our Children Need – And What We Can Do About It,* "Schools haven't changed; the world has. And so our schools are not failing. Rather, they are obsolete—even the ones that score the best on standardized tests. This is a very different problem requiring an altogether different solution."

Objectives:

- ⮑ Explain how the world transformed by technology requires students to possess new knowledge, skills, and dispositions for the 21st-century economy.
- ⮑ Identify 21st-century skills and why they are essential for today's learners.
- ⮑ Describe why students need to possess digital literacy to be successful in the modern workplace.

1.1 The World is Changing Quickly

Over the last twenty years, the standards-based "reforms" driven by high-stakes testing have taken the nation's education system in the wrong direction. Instead of looking backward and trying to prepare our students for a world and economy that no longer exists, we should be preparing them for the world to come. Author and futurist Buckminster Fuller created the "knowledge doubling curve" when he noticed that until the 20th-century human knowledge doubled approximately every century. By the end of World War II, however, knowledge was doubling every twenty-five years. Today, on average, human knowledge is doubling every thirteen months. And according to IBM, the development of the "Internet of Things" will lead to a doubling of all knowledge every twelve hours. This incredible growth in information is due to the evolution of the Internet. In 1995 there were approximately 16 million users worldwide. By the end of 2019, there were 4.6 billion Internet users, almost two-thirds of the world's population. With the increase in online users, social media has exploded. In 2019 there were 3.7 billion users. According to research conducted by Global WebIndex, "Social media users are now spending an average of 2 hours and 24 minutes per day multi networking across an average of 8 social networks and messaging apps." E-commerce is quickly dominating the retail market and has increased dramatically, going from 1.6 billion users in 2017 to 2 billion in 2019, which is a quarter of the world's population now shopping online. And according to Nasdaq, those numbers will only increase. By 2040, consumers will make 95 percent of all purchases online.

According to the World Economic Forum, the most sought-after occupations in many industrialized nations did not exist ten or even five years ago. Careers such as digital marketing specialist, social media manager, chief listening officer, blogger, search engine optimization specialist, app designer, cloud services specialist, big data analyst, and market research data miner, to name a few. One popular estimate predicts that 65 percent of children entering primary school today will ultimately work in jobs that don't currently exist. Richard Riley, Bill Clinton's secretary of education, once pointed out, "We are currently preparing students for the jobs that don't yet exist ... using technologies that haven't been invented ... in order to solve problems we don't even know are problems yet."

The modern technological revolution spurred on by the microprocessor, personal computers, the Internet, and smartphones has fundamentally changed how we live and work. Not since Guttenberg's printing press has there been greater democratization of knowledge and information. Anyone with a device and Internet connection can access almost unlimited information anytime and anywhere, regardless of their social and economic status. Big tech such as Apple, Microsoft, Amazon, Google, and Facebook has become the new big business of the 21st century. Much like the railroads, oil, chemical, and steel manufacturers were of the 19th and 20th centuries. In his book *The World is Flat: A Brief History of the Twenty-First Century*, Thomas Friedman describes how technology has fundamentally leveled the economic playing field. Friedman points out that flatteners such as the Internet, broadband, online workflow software, and collaboration have contributed to outsourcing service jobs to countries that can most efficiently and cost-effectively perform the task. In other words, today's high school and college graduates are not just competing with other graduates from the same towns, cities, and states, but with workers around the world in a new digital global workplace. And while technology has fundamentally changed most aspects of life, the way we educate our children has remained stubbornly rooted in the past.

The modern American school is the product of its industrial past that emphasized conformity and efficiency. Students are grouped according to age and not ability, bells signal when classes begin and end, and strict enforcement of punctuality and classroom discipline are the norm. Schools organize courses by subject, and teachers evaluate students by letter grades and points and not mastery of content. Most teachers use direct instruction to present information to the class, relying heavily on the textbook to drive their curriculum. Students sitting in neatly arranged rows and columns dutifully take notes and memorize what the teachers taught. In the early 20th century, students would "toe the line" or recite the lessons from memory. Today, most teachers assess student learning with standardized tests that consist of multiple-choice, true and false, matching, and short answer questions. Fill in the bubble assessments are among the most common forms of assessment used in schools. They are quick to create, administer, evaluate, and are theoretically free from bias (see chapter 2 for a thorough explanation of authentic assessment). The problems associated with these tests are well documented but continue to proliferate at all education levels. Federal legislation, such as the No Child Left Behind Act and Every Student Succeeds Act, has put intense pressure on students to perform well on high-stakes standardized tests. High-stakes standardized testing has resulted in a significant narrowing of the curriculum and usurpation of time and energy to focus on testable subjects such as reading and mathematics. Meanwhile, non-testable but equally essential subjects like social studies, foreign languages, art, and music do not receive the attention they deserve.

TEACHING STRATEGY:

I love popular music, and I try to inject it whenever possible into my curriculum. I enjoy introducing my students to music, songs, and styles such as blues, jazz, roots music, country, rock 'n' roll, rap and metal, and everything in between. As a U.S. history teacher, music helps me teach American cultural history as I select songs that illuminate the period of study, such as 1960s protest songs against the war in Vietnam. Additionally, music helps me build relationships with my students and is an excellent "hook" to draw students into learning by generating excitement and energy for the lesson. Additionally, using music is a perfect way to teach rhetorical analysis by examining the song's lyrics and using storytelling as a vehicle for teaching and learning. Music also activates students' emotions, which is directly related to memory and learning. My favorite online resources include Flocabulary https://www. flocabulary.com/, Rock n roll Hall of Fame Free Online Learning https:// www.rockhall.com/education, Teach Rock https://teachrock.org/, and Teaching Context with Album Covers https://lessonplans.dwrl.utexas. edu/content/teaching-context-album-covers.html.

Rote memorization may have been appropriate to an agricultural and industrial-based economy but is anachronistic in the modern technological world. While a high degree of technical ability is needed to succeed in the modern workforce, today's employers look for candidates who possess technical and soft skills. Soft skills are personal attributes that are necessary for success in the workplace. Recently the World Economic Forum released a paper titled *The Future of Jobs Report: 2020*. The report documented the top fifteen skills for 2025. They are:

1. Analytical thinking and innovation
2. Active learning and learning strategies
3. Complex problem-solving
4. Critical thinking and analysis
5. Creativity, originality, and initiative
6. Leadership and social influence
7. Technology use, monitoring, and control
8. Technology design and programing
9. Resilience, stress tolerance, and flexibility
10. Reasoning, problem-solving, and ideation
11. Emotional intelligence
12. Troubleshooting and user experience
13. Service orientation
14. Systems analysis and evaluation
15. Persuasion and negotiation.

Employers are looking for candidates who know how to learn independently, solve problems creatively, innovate, communicate, and collaborate. In addition, workers need to self-regulate, have a high degree of emotional intelligence, and work with others from diverse backgrounds. Unfortunately, there is a growing schism between what schools do and what employers need. This gap only increases as new technologies develop, such as artificial intelligence, autonomous vehicles, robotics, and green technology. Schools can help prepare their students for the modern world and the future by utilizing 21st-century skills in all aspects of the curriculum.

1.2 21st Century Skills for the Knowledge Economy

A knowledge economy is one that is dependent on the knowledge and skills of its workers to create and innovate. Twenty-first-century skills are the skills and dispositions that students will need to succeed in the knowledge economy to include college, career, and civic life. Researchers from Harvard University define 21st-century skills as the "production and services based on knowledge-intensive activities that contribute to an accelerated pace of technical and scientific advance, as well as rapid obsolescence. The key component of a knowledge economy is a greater reliance on intellectual capabilities than on physical inputs or natural resources" (Powell & Snellman, 2004).

Teachers can apply these skills to any grade level, academic discipline, and in all career and civic settings. Twenty-first-century skills can be grouped into three overarching categories:

Learning Skills

Learning skills are necessary to cultivate a person's creative potential and include the 4 C's: creativity and innovation, critical thinking and problem-solving, effective communication, and collaboration.

Digital Literacy Skills

These skills help students become responsible consumers and creators of digital content. They help students locate, evaluate, and process new information and create content for the web.

Life Skills

These are the skills that enable students to live productive well-rounded lives both in their personal lives and as members of work teams. The skills include adaptability, initiative, leadership and responsibility, productivity, cross-cultural understanding, and social awareness.

TEACHING STRATEGY:

One of the best ways to provide students with opportunities to learn and practice 21st-century skills is by implementing project-based learning or PBL. According to PBLWorks, one of the leading authorities on PBL, "PBL is a teaching method in which students gain knowledge and skills by working for an extended period to investigate and respond to an authentic, engaging, and complex question, problem, or challenge." PBL is not to be confused with traditional school projects. Traditional projects are usually assigned at the end of a unit of study as a form of enrichment. PBL, on the other hand, is the primary mode of student learning. In other words, PBL is the "main course" and not just the "dessert." The advantage of PBL is that teachers across grade levels and subject disciplines can adapt PBL to suit the individual needs of their students. In other words, PBL can look very different from one classroom to another. It is the flexibility to adapt PBL to students' individual needs that PBL derives its power. However, despite PBL's tractability, according to PBLWorks, there are seven generally accepted components of all PBL lessons. Projects must address a challenging problem or question, students must be engaged in iterative sustained inquiry, the project must be authentic and have real-world applicability, students must have voice and choice in the PBL process, there must be opportunities for reflection and critique, and finally, the PBL must conclude with a public presentation of students' final products, usually before an audience of community stakeholders and experts.

The research supporting the effectiveness of PBL is emerging but promising. An analysis of four literature reviews spanning thirty years in various academic subjects concludes that PBL can promote student learning and has the potential to be more effective than traditional approaches in social studies, science, mathematics, and literacy, especially for disadvantaged students (Kingston, 2018). PBL is beneficial for college preparatory students too. A recent randomized study spanning over two years involving 3,635 students in five urban school districts revealed that students who took Advanced Placement courses that utilized PBL and Knowledge in Action (KIA) approaches scored eight percentage points higher on Advanced Placement U.S. Government and Politics and Environmental Science exams, than students who took traditional Advanced Placement courses (Saavedra et al., 2021). Additionally, research has shown that PBL strengthens students' 21st-century skills such as critical thinking, collaboration (Evans, 2020), complex communication (Thompson, 2020), and self-directed learning (Brandt, 2020). Additionally, according to PBLWorks, "Teachers who often assign creative, project-based activities are more likely than other teachers to say their students display a range of learning and development goals, including building self-confidence, utilizing their unique strengths, and developing critical thinking and problem-solving skills."

As a high school U.S. history teacher, I love to engage my classes with the National History Day (NHD) curriculum. NHD is an excellent way to get history students in grades 7–12 involved in the PBL. Plus, it is a perfect entry point to doing PBL due to the abundance of resources provided for free by NHD. Every year NHD publishes an annual theme that students must address in the creation of their projects. NHD requires students to ask their own questions and search for their own answers by conducting primary and secondary research. Then students construct a final product to communicate their research conclusions. Students can select to create an exhibit board, website, documentary video, research paper, or performance. Students can participate in NHD as individuals or as members of a collaborative team. Think of NHD as a science fair for history students.

Many schools, districts, and states have NHD fairs in which students have the opportunity to present their final projects to their classmates, families, and members of the community. NHD winners are selected based on the quality of their final projects to include an annotated bibliography, process paper, and an interview with judges. Winners of their state-level competitions can compete in the national competition held at the University of Maryland in the summer. When students create a project for competition, I have found that it raises the stakes that go beyond typical school busywork like worksheets and review questions. Students rise to the occasion and do incredible work because the work is relevant, personal, and sustained. NHD has been proven to elevate students' academic achievement across all academic subjects, including reading, writing, and mathematics. Additionally, NHD prepares students for college, career, and citizenship by teaching students the 21st-century skills they will need to succeed (Sloan & Rockman, 2011).

Despite the benefits of PBL, there are significant challenges to the approach. The first is the training that teachers need to implement PBL effectively. Because it is a paradigm shift from traditional teaching methods such as direct instruction, teachers will need to become familiar with PBL approaches. Proficiency in teaching PBL can take months and even years to master. Teachers must methodically plan projects to create the essential question, develop a project plan and schedule, prepare assessments and evaluations (formative and summative), and reflect. In PBL, teachers serve as a "guide on the side," helping students to answer their own questions, conduct research, and plan and create their projects. Further, teachers assist students to manage their time, set goals, and work productively in cooperative learning groups. At times, teachers may also have to motivate and encourage students through the challenging PBL process helping students develop grit and perseverance.

Another drawback of PBL is that many teachers believe it to be too time-consuming and experience frustration trying to fit PBL into an already dense school day. PBL requires teachers to rethink their curriculum and understand that student-centered learning approaches inherently take longer to implement. Still, the tradeoff in student learning and achievement makes PBL a good investment of time. Surprisingly, many students will push back on PBL at first because PBL will transfer the hard work of learning from the teacher to the students. Students may also feel anxiety when involved in learning tasks that do not have a clear "right" answer. For example, one of my standard retorts to student questions is, "What does your analysis of the evidence suggest?" Even though teaching PBL is time-consuming and involved, I know that my students have grown as researchers, critical thinkers, and communicators. In addition to the academic growth I have seen my students make due to PBL, the looks of pride and accomplishment on their faces when they submit their final projects are priceless. When I engage my students with PBL, I create lifelong independent learners who have the skills and dispositions to succeed as students, employees, and citizens.

CREATIVITY AND INNOVATION: THE CURRENCY OF THE KNOWLEDGE ECONOMY

Creativity and innovation have become the currency of the 21st-century workforce. A whole cottage industry of business books has emerged to teach the secrets of creative and innovative thinking. *Titles such as Originals, Think Big, The Winner's Brain, The Creativity Code, and Habit* have become mandatory reading for those trying to gain an edge in a fiercely competitive marketplace. Creativity and innovation are often used interchangeably, and while they are related, they are two separate things. In his book *Out Think: How Innovative Leaders Drive Exceptional Outcomes*, Shawn Hunter defines creativity as "the capability or act of conceiving something original or unusual." Creative people defy the status quo. They see the world differently and approach novel situations in new and unusual ways. The "creative class" makes up about 30 percent of the American workforce today. They hail from various professions, including engineers, managers, academics, researchers, designers, entrepreneurs, lawyers, and programmers. Creative, "outside of the box" thinkers are in demand because the world is changing so fast that old procedural ways of looking at the world have become an anachronism in the knowledge economy. Creative people do not see the world as it is, but it could be a prerequisite to innovative thinking.

Hunter describes innovation as "the implementation or creation of something new that has realized value to others." Innovation is usually realized as some sort of tool that is used to solve problems or create opportunities. America's rise to worldwide economic hegemony has resulted from innovators over the centuries who have made the technologies to drive America's economic engine. Benjamin Franklin, Alexander Graham Bell, Thomas Edison, George Washington Carver, the Wright brothers, Bill Gates, and Steve Jobs, to name a few. America's ability to create innovative thinkers has been one of its strengths. We must continue to produce individuals who will push the boundaries of possibility. Innovation results from individuals and teams who think outside of the box creatively and in new ways. These disruptors are not afraid to challenge the status quo and see possibilities where others see defeat. According to Tony Wagner in his book *Creating Innovators: The Making of Young People Who Will Change the World*, innovators possess specific characteristics. They have a lot of curiosity and are continually learning about the world around them. They seek knowledge from a wide variety of diverse topics. They ask questions and want to understand subjects deeply. Innovators are collaborators. They actively listen to others' points of view, especially those they disagree with, to gain new perspectives and points of view. Innovators are not afraid to take action. They experiment and try new approaches to move forward. They are not afraid to make mistakes and see failure as an opportunity rather than a setback. As the adage goes, "If at first, you don't succeed, try, try again."

Sir Ken Robinson's 2006 TED talk, "Do Schools Kill Creativity?", with almost 20 million views, is one of the most-watched TED talks on YouTube. In it, Robinson argues that American public schools squander children's remarkable talents for creativity and innovation by basing the education system solely on academic ability. By prioritizing academic subjects like mathematics and reading over the humanities and arts, schools expunge human beings' natural curiosity and creativity. "We are educating people out of their creative capacities." Schools do this when they teach students that there can only be one right answer. Creativity is diminished when they stress math and literacy to the detriment of the arts. Schools teach students that failure is wrong and is something to be avoided. As a result, students learn to avoid taking risks in exchange for the comfort of conformity. These factors contribute to the decline of creativity in schools.

Robinson goes on to argue that "creativity is as important today in education as literacy, and we should treat it with the same status." Recent research suggests that educators can teach creativity under the right circumstances. Therefore, schools today should foster creativity and innovative thinking as a priority. As the author Sir Antony Jay once wrote, "The uncreative mind can spot wrong answers, but it takes a very creative mind to spot wrong questions." Understanding the importance of creativity, in 2001, a group of cognitive psychologists, curriculum theorists, and assessment researchers published *A Taxonomy for Teaching, Learning, and Assessment*. This was an update to the iconic Bloom's taxonomy of learning, which mapped out six domains of cognitive processes. The updated version places creativity at the pinnacle of all learning.

Writing for the Harvard Business Review, Professor Teresa M. Amabile suggests that individual creativity and innovation consists of three interrelated components; namely, expertise, creative thinking skills, and motivation. Expertise is essential to innovation, especially when it comes from the combined knowledge of a wide range of networked experts. Creative thinking skills involve thinking about problems in new ways. Motivation, however, plays an integral role in developing creative and innovative individuals. Human motivation can be broken down into two significant categories: extrinsic motivation and intrinsic motivation. Extrinsic motivation is the result of external punishments and rewards. For example, most students do their schoolwork not because they find it exciting and engaging. Instead, they are trying to avoid a penalty for failure to do so. Additionally, students may be seeking external rewards such as praise, recognition, or good grades. External motivation is sometimes thought of in terms of the carrot and the stick as extrinsically motivated individuals are acted upon by forces outside of themselves.

Internal motivation is when individuals are motivated to do something because they enjoy the activity and find great satisfaction. According to Kenneth Thomas in his book *Intrinsic Motivation at Work: What Drives Employee Engagement*, there are four sources of intrinsic motivation; namely, meaningfulness, choice, competence, and progress. Meaningfulness means that the work has personal relevance. Work without purpose is akin to Sisyphus rolling the rock up the hill in Hades, only to have it roll back, repeating the cycle over and over for eternity. Second, individuals should have the ability to make choices about their work. Instead of forcing a one-size-fits-all approach on everyone, individuals should exercise a degree of agency regarding what and how they accomplish. Third, individuals must feel competent in what they are doing; they are doing well with a high degree of satisfaction and pride. Frequent and meaningful feedback of work can help them feel competent that what they are doing is essential. Lastly, individuals should have a sense of progress. They must believe that what they are doing matters. They are contributing to something greater than themselves and have growing confidence in their abilities.

TEACHING STRATEGY:

Creativity is an essential 21st-century skill, but teachers are often perplexed by how to teach it. The good news is that almost any learning activity that gives students voice and choice will help students develop their creativity. As Dan Pink, the author of *Drive: The Surprising Truth About What Motivates Us*, points out, when people have a sense of autonomy, mastery, and purpose, they will have the freedom and inner drive to develop genuinely creative solutions. As discussed earlier, PBL is a fantastic way to develop students' creativity because it gives students agency, the opportunity to become experts on their given topic, and allows students to tackle real-world issues relevant to their lives.

Another strategy to develop students' creativity is to have them keep a "da Vinci journal." Leonardo da Vinci filled over thirteen thousand notebook pages with observations, ideas, sketches, notes, designs, doodles, questions, and calculations. Thinking and journaling daily, da Vinci nurtured his creativity over a lifetime, coming up with inventions such as the flying machine, parachute, diving suit, shoes for walking on water, armored tank, machine gun, and the robotic knight. Creativity can be grown, but it must be developed over time with intentionality, just like any other skill. Help students develop their creativity by getting them in the daily habit of jotting down their ideas, curiosities, and questions.

Additionally, teachers can help students become more creative by implementing a "genius hour." A genius hour is when the teacher sets aside an hour or more a week so that students can engage in passion projects, usually unrelated to an academic subject. There are many different ways to implement the genius hour, but generally speaking, students must start with an essential question or problem that cannot be answered with a simple Google search. Students will then research to answer their questions. And finally, students must create a final product by publishing, designing, producing, or providing a service.

1.3 Critical Thinking & Problem-Solving: Essential Skills for Today's Workforce

Albert Einstein once said, "We cannot solve our problems with the same thinking we used when we created them." Einstein's words were prescient as critical thinking and problem-solving quickly became the most sought-after "soft skills" in the job market. According to the *Wall Street Journal*, the number of job postings that mention "critical thinking" as a desired skill has doubled since 2009. Indeed.com, one of the nation's leading job search sites, found that over 21,000 health care and 6,700 management positions contained references to the skill. The Fourth Industrial Revolution, powered by rapid advancements and consolidation of artificial intelligence and machine learning technologies, robotics, nanotechnology, 3D printing, genetics, and biotechnology, will significantly disrupt the global workplace. A recent report published by the World Economic Forum titled *The Future of Jobs* revealed that human resource officers from leading international employers cite complex problem-solving and critical thinking as the two most essential skills for 2020. And while these skills are difficult to define, according to the Foundation for Critical Thinking, critical thinking is "that mode of thinking—about any subject, content, or problem—in which the thinker improves the quality of his or her thinking by skillfully taking charge of the structures inherent in thinking and imposing intellectual standards upon them." In other words, critical thinkers can articulate the exact nature of a problem. They gather and assess information and interpret it to come to conclusions and solutions, testing them against relevant standards. Critical thinkers are open-minded and entertain alternative systems of thought while continually challenging their assumptions and bias. And they can effectively communicate while trying to figure out solutions to complex problems.

Critical thinking and problem-solving are essential skills for the 21st-century knowledge economy because the proliferation of information requires individuals to possess the ability to make decisions and judgments about data. In other words, individuals must learn to think clearly, and analytically to solve complex problems in a milieu that increasingly requires flexible intellectual skills.

According to a recent article published by Ziprecruiter.com titled "Why Critical Thinking Skills Are Important in the Workplace," critical thinking is a learned skill, not just an automatic response possessed by all human beings. Most people go about their lives thinking in uncritical ways. For example, they make personal and professional decisions based on biases, self-interests, and unexamined emotions and ideologies. *Harvard Business Review* offers three approaches to grow one's aptitude in critical thinking and problem-solving. First, question personal assumptions. When we do this, we look beyond conventional wisdom and challenge our own beliefs and examine all possible alternatives in a given situation. Don't assume everything you think you know is right. Keep an open mind, and always strive to learn more about the world around you. Second, apply rational thought and logical thinking to problem-solving. Human beings frequently fall into the familiar trap of assuming they know why things are the way they are, often allowing unexamined correlations to pass for causation. When one does not exist, assuming a cause-and-effect relationship stifles out-of-the-box thinking and the ability to solve complex problems. Finally, seek out diversity of thought and collaborate with others whenever possible. Working with diverse teams of people helps us break out of familiar ways of seeing the world. They allow us to challenge assumptions, the status quo, and groupthink. Diversity is important because we are likely to associate with people like us, living in the proverbial "bubble" of conformity, safety, and comfort.

Because critical thinking skills are essential in the 21st-century knowledge economy, some argue that requiring students to memorize information is anathema to complex cognitive processes. This point of view is held by many who point out that most students have access to smartphones and computers and can simply look up information anytime, anywhere, making memorization of content moot. However tempting as it may be to minimize the importance of learned material, there is value in memorization. Like muscles in the body, the brain must undergo regular exercise, or it atrophies. Memorization strengthens the brain by increasing and strengthening neural pathways through repetition. Subsequently, the learned content establishes a base of knowledge in long-term memory. This frees up short-term memory so that it can learn new things. Further, it is impossible to think critically about things you do not know. As cognitive scientists Lauren Resnick and Megan Hall point out, "What we know now is that just as facts do not constitute true knowledge and thinking power, so thinking processes cannot proceed without something to think about." In other words, schools must provide students both the content and the skills to think about their learning critically.

TEACHING STRATEGY: CRITICAL THINKING

Critical thinking can be taught to students. A review of 341 studies revealed "that there are effective strategies for teaching critical thinking skills, both generic and content-specific, and critical thinking dispositions, at all educational levels and across all disciplinary areas" (Abrami et al., 2015). Of course, critical thinking is a complex subject that has many different components. Still, a direct and straightforward way teachers can help their students become critical thinkers is to encourage students to ask their own questions and to be skeptical of claims of fact or conventional wisdom. I like to ask students, "How do you know that is true?" "What is your source of evidence?" "Can your source be trusted?"

1.4 Communication and Collaboration: Critical Skills for the 21st Century Economy

Researchers continue to debate how long human beings have been able to talk with one another—estimates for the use of oral language range from fifty thousand to two million years ago. Writing is a much newer phenomenon and can be traced back to ancient Mesopotamia, beginning in 3400 BCE with the cuneiform writing system. Thus, oral and written communications are not precisely new skills. Still, they are just important today as they have been throughout history. A Pew Research Center poll of American adults revealed that they believe communication is an essential skill for all students "to get ahead in the world today." The emphasis of these skills is because a person's ability to communicate effectively orally and in writing is a fundamental component of most careers at all levels and is essential to the successful transmission of ideas from one person to another and groups of people.

Effective written communication involves knowing the rules of English grammar, spelling, and punctuation. The most obvious reason to use Standard American English is that incorrect grammar and spelling adversely affect your credibility with readers. Readers may make assumptions about the writer's intelligence or education levels or believe the writer does not care if the message contains errors. For example, a billboard from a technical college advertised, "Be a Biomedical Technician." While this is a simple mistake, future students will likely question the credibility of higher learning institutions that overlook spelling errors. In the often-cited example, "Let's eat Grandma!" instead of "Let's eat, Grandma!" The comma can make the difference between an exhortation to dinner or having grandma as the main course. Bad grammar could even affect your love life! A study of 1,700 adult online dates found that 43 percent of users consider lousy grammar decidedly unattractive, and 35 percent think good grammar is appealing.

Further, good writing could make the difference between getting a job or not. A recent hiring managers survey revealed that 86 percent of them would not hire applicants who had grammar mistakes on their résumé or cover letters. It is interesting to note that many search engines punish content with grammar and spelling errors by pushing it down in its search results. As a senior product manager for Bing pointed out, "Just as you're judging others' writing, so the engines judge yours. If you struggle to get past typos, why would an engine show a page of content with errors higher in the rankings when other pages of error-free content exist to serve the searcher? Like it or not, we're judged by the quality of the results we show. So we are constantly watching the quality of the content we see."

In addition to using English grammar effectively, communicators must be aware of who will be reading their content. "Know your audience" is one of the cardinal rules of good writing because it informs the kind of voice writers use. It is crucial to understand that an appropriate communication style with family and friends may not suit a professional setting. Writing a text message or social media post is very different than writing a professional email or memo. In the former, texting abbreviations, emojis, and slang is expected but inappropriate in the latter. Writers need to articulate their ideas clearly and succinctly so that the author's meaning is transmitted effectively, leaving little room for ambiguity and interpretation. Good communicators should be able to express logical arguments based on evidence clearly and concisely. Additionally, effective communication is the foundation of successful collaboration because it allows for building relationships. Good relationships allow for productive collaboration.

TEACHING STRATEGY:

Students should have as many opportunities as possible to write across all disciplines in various styles. The research supports this conclusion. A recent meta-analysis of fifty-six studies examining the benefits of writing in social studies, science, and math found that when students write, they "reliably enhanced learning" because writing requires that students be able to recall and organize information, synthesize what they have learned, and make connections between various concepts, which helps students retain information in long-term memory (Graham, Kiuhara, & MacKay, 2020). In English and social studies classes writing is usually expository, descriptive, persuasive, and reflective. In STEM fields, the writing is more technical such as that used in lab reports. Regardless of the subject, students should be taught to write clearly and precisely in a way that is engaging and interesting. As physicist and mathematician Max Born pointed out in his book *My Life and My Views* (1968), "To present a scientific subject in an attractive and stimulating manner is an artistic task, similar to that of a novelist or even a dramatic writer." Teachers in both the humanities and STEM disciplines should teach their students the 6+1 traits of good writing.

Ideas — Writing has clear main ideas and includes sufficient supporting details; writing shows, and not just tells.

Organization — Information is presented in a logical way that has a discernable beginning, middle, and end.

Voice — Personal tone or personality that permeates the writing. Must be appropriate for the subject, purpose, and audience.

Word Choice — Nouns and verbs are used precisely. The writer avoids slang, colloquiums, and jargon. All technical language is clearly defined.

Fluency — Various sentence lengths and composition impact the rhythm and flow of the writing.

Conventions — Follow the rules of standard English in terms of capitalization, punctuation, spelling, and grammar.

Presentation — How the writing is presented, including fonts, colors, images and graphics, lists, and tables, must be appropriate for the writing's subject, audience, and purpose.

▌COLLABORATION

In the industrial past, machines replaced skilled artisans in the mass production of consumer goods. The assembly line reduced manufacturing into small repetitive tasks requiring workers to perform for twelve to sixteen hours a day, six days a week. Factory supervisors enforced strict discipline to keep workers productive by limiting bathroom breaks and mealtimes. Talking between employees was forbidden. The 21st-century knowledge economy requires a new kind of worker, much different from its industrial predecessor. Today's workplace requires a workforce that must collaborate effectively as members of teams both in person and across networks. Teamwork and collaboration are essential because they have been indelibly linked to organizational success. Collaboration promotes problem-solving, boosts learning and sharing skills, increases employee satisfaction and productivity, and spurs innovation. The popular image of the lone inventor tinkering in the garage to create the next significant innovation may have been true in certain limited cases. Still, today and tomorrow's breakthroughs will result from the collaborative efforts of teams of people. As the author of *The One Minute Manager, Kenneth Blanchard*, once wrote, "None of us is as smart as all of us." For example, the Department of Energy's network of National Laboratories has advanced supercomputing, decoded DNA, kick-started the development of the worldwide web in North America, powered NASA spacecraft, harnessed the atom's power, invented new materials, mapped the universe and the dark side of the moon, confirmed the Big Bang, and discovered dark energy, just to name a few of its achievements. None of these discoveries and innovations was achieved in isolation. Instead, they were all the results of teams of researchers and scientists working together to find solutions to complex problems.

TEACHING STRATEGY:

Teachers should never assume that students know how to collaborate in small learning groups effectively. Even though collaborative learning has been around for a long time, the skills and dispositions needed to succeed in this approach may have never been taught to students. Therefore, teachers must be deliberate in organizing and structuring learning groups to meet the objectives of the lesson or activity. There are seven things teachers must consider when creating small collaborative learning groups.

1. **Deliberately Select which Students will Work Together**

   The old expression "birds of a feather flock together" accurately describes what will happen when students are left on their own to select their learning groups, which means that they are likely to choose partners who have similar interests and points of view. Depending on the activity, this may be an appropriate strategy. However, if a teacher wants diverse perspectives, personalities, motivation, and abilities, they must make a conscious effort to create diverse student groups.

2. **Group Size**

   Group size is not fixed, but research indicates that groups of between five and six students are optimal for learning gains in collaborative learning. In contrast, groups larger than eight are not effective (Kooloos et al., 2011). In this range, students reported higher motivation, cohesiveness, intellectual development through analysis of each other's arguments and points of view, and the ability to express themselves and their ideas freely.

3. **Listening Skills**

   Hearing is not a skill, but listening is. Teach students how to effectively listen, including making eye contact, monitoring their body language, not interrupting the speaker, and repeating back to the speaker their main ideas. The most effective way to teach students this skill is by modeling it for them. Role-play with a student what effective and ineffective communication looks like. They are more likely to learn the skill after seeing it than simply being told what it is.

4. **Rules of Collaboration**

   Almost always, there will be a few students in each group who will demonstrate natural leadership abilities, and they will be inclined to take over the group. Teach students how to collaborate by providing them with conflict resolution skills, active listening, and empathetic concern. Teach students how to build on the ideas of others and to value the contributions, no matter how small, of all group members.

5. **Make Goals and Expectations Clear**

   Anytime the teacher puts students in learning groups, there must be clear goals and expectations for the meeting. If not, the group will become distracted and turn into a social event. I like to project a presentation slide that has the objectives for the class. This way, they can refer to it throughout collaboration time.

6. **Assign Group Roles**

   This may be one of the most critical steps in forming effective small groups. When you assign students a role in the group, they should be clear about what they are supposed to do. One of the main reasons why groups fail is due to confusion and lack of direction. Be proactive and assign, or let students select their group roles. Roles can be rotated or stay static throughout the activity. The leader will direct the group during the lesson and maintain open communication between group members and the teacher. The recorder will keep notes of the group's decisions and submit any written assignments. The motivator keeps the group positive by limiting negative talk, giving words of encouragement and praise. The editor is responsible for proofreading all work so that it is free of errors. Depending on the assignment, other roles may include the researcher, timekeeper, and presenter.

7. **Group, Peer, and Self-Assessment**

   One of the biggest pushbacks against collaborative learning from students is the way group work is assessed. Nothing is as offensive to students' sense of fairness as a student getting a grade they did not earn. To avoid students "hiding" or riding on the coattails of other students' work, teachers must hold all students accountable. When engaged in collaborative learning, both the individual and the group should be evaluated. Evaluating individual contributions to a group project can be tricky because it is not always apparent who did what. For these reasons, I like to have my students evaluate their contributions to the project and the contributions of their colleagues. I have students do their evaluations in secret because they are more inclined to provide an honest assessment of their peers' contributions if the identity of the evaluator is not known. In addition to evaluating the final product, it is crucial to consider the process. In other words, knowing how well students worked together to accomplish a final goal is a significant component of 21st-century learning. Additionally, all rubrics and grading criteria should be shared with students before they begin the learning tasks. That way, students know exactly what the expectations for the project are and how they will be evaluated. While far from perfect, using rubrics will help to mitigate bias and create more consistency in the grading process.

1.5 Digital Literacy the New Essential Skill

Today's students are digital natives. That is, they were born into a world that has always known personal computers, the Internet, smartphones, and digital gaming. As a result, many assume that these children are highly proficient in their use. Unfortunately, this could be further from the truth. A multiyear study conducted by Learning.com revealed that 75 percent of fifth and eighth graders are non-proficient in 21st-century skills. The study involved over 110,000 students who took the 21st Century Skills Assessment from 2012 to 2017, which measured the digital literacy skills in the International Society for Technology in Education standards or ISTE. According to Learning.com C.E.O., Keith Oelrich, "When we look at the test scores for this significant sample of students, it is alarming to see that the vast majority of fifth and eighth-graders did not have the digital skills necessary for success in college and their future careers—not to mention high school, which is right around the corner."

The American Library Association's digital literacy task force defines digital literacy as "The ability to use information and communication technologies to find, evaluate, create, and communicate information, requiring both cognitive and technical skills." Professor of literacy and technology at North Carolina State, Hiller Spires, points out that digital literacy consists of three major components: (1) finding and consuming digital content, (2) creating digital content, and (3) communicating or sharing it. A recent report indicates that teens spend, on average, seven hours and twenty-two minutes a day on their phones. That time consists of mostly watching videos and playing games and does not include screen time for schoolwork. While young people might be competent at finding and consuming entertainment online, they cannot distinguish between commercially influenced sources and peer-reviewed and academic sources. In addition, the so-called "Google generation" often lacks the patience and knowledge to conduct meaningful Internet searches, as demonstrated by the fact that less than 10 percent of searchers click "Next" beyond Google's first page of results.

The democratization of the Internet, including the proliferation of Web 2.0 or the social web, has enabled Internet users to create, distribute, and interact with original content on blogs, wikis, folksonomies, video, photo sharing sites, and other social media. Over one thousand new websites are created every minute of every day. While many users do so for altruistic purposes, some misuse the technology to do harm. For example, in 2016, the Pew Research Center conducted a study just after the presidential election. They found that 64 percent of adults believed that fake news stories caused a great deal of confusion. Twenty-three percent of respondents reported that they had shared fake news stories online. While most had done so unintentionally, some admitted to doing so on purpose. A recent Stanford University study examined middle school, high school, and university students' ability to assess the Internet's information. The results indicate that students have difficulty understanding how to evaluate content for bias, reliability, and veracity. According to the study, "Many assume that because young people are fluent in social media, they are equally savvy about what they find there, our work shows the opposite." For example, more than 80 percent of middle schoolers believed that "sponsored content" was the equivalent of a real news story. In addition, most high school students blindly accepted photographs as presented without verifying or challenging them, not understanding that images can be manipulated to influence public opinion.

Additionally, they couldn't tell the difference between a fake news story and a real one on Facebook. The study found that most college students could not detect bias in a tweet from an activist group with a discernable political agenda. Even students from Stanford, one of the nation's most elite colleges, could not correctly identify the difference between mainstream and fringe sources found online. Taken together, these findings indicate that our students are not equipped to critically evaluate and consume online information, which can have serious educational, political, economic, and personal consequences. Digital literacy will become increasingly more critical as technology continues to evolve. For example, individuals use artificial intelligence and deep learning technology to create video forgeries known as deepfakes. Deepfakes essentially transpose real and fictional faces onto actors creating realistic videos that appear true to life. Deepfakes have a wide range of practical purposes, such as restoring old video footage, resurrecting deceased actors to reprise roles in new movies, and creating personal avatars to be used in professional settings. Retailers have even designed apps that use deepfake technology so that users can try on new clothes, eyeglasses, and hairstyles. And while the technology used by major movie studios and retailers is expensive and not accessible to the general public, less costly apps have been created, allowing anyone to create authentic-looking deepfake videos. Just as all technology can be used for good and evil, deepfakes have the potential to be used for fraudulent purposes. That is why educators must teach students the skills to analyze content and to identify dubious content critically.

TEACHING STRATEGY:

There are steps that teachers can take to help their students become more critical consumers of online content. According to Evaluating Wikipedia, Internet users should ask themselves the following questions. First, who is the author of the website? Are they qualified to write on a given topic? Do they have professional credentials? If no author is listed, what does the domain name or web address reveal about the website? Second, students should ask themselves what the intended purpose of the website is? Was it created to inform, explain, persuade, or sell a product? Students should have the skills to know how to tell the difference. Also, students should be able to discern objectivity. In other words, they should know if the information presented is a fact, opinion, or propaganda. They need to understand how to detect bias from language and how the information is presented. Third, students ask themselves if the information is accurate? Does the website contradict what they already know about a given topic? Are there links to source information so that the content can be verified beyond the website? Has the content been peer-reviewed or refereed? Finally, students should question the credibility of the source. In other words, can the information contained on the website be trusted? Does it come from a reputable source such as a university, government, or an established and trusted company or industry? Is the website current, has it been recently updated? Do all of the links work? Do they lead to reputable sources of information? Does the website contain spelling and grammatical errors that might indicate the site was created for nefarious purposes? Students must develop the habits of mind to ask critical questions about all information consumed online and in the disconnected world to become savvy consumers of digital content.

CONTENT CREATORS

Today's students do not only need to know how to find and evaluate sources of information, but they must be proficient at creating and disseminating content. There are many reasons why students should become digital content creators. One is the pride students take in creating something authentic and relevant. Unlike physical projects like poster boards, shoebox dioramas, and research papers, online content can be seen by multitudes of people worldwide. When students have the opportunity to create digital artifacts, they feel a sense of ownership, purpose, and importance because they know their content could be seen by a greater audience beyond the classroom walls. Additionally, creating digital content will allow interactions between the creator and the consumer that might challenge their points of view, the status quo, and conventional ways of thinking. These interactions are essential, particularly in heterogeneous classrooms that don't have the opportunity to hear diverse perspectives. Creating digital content, such as blogs, vlogs, digital books, memes, documentary and explainer videos, and slideshows, to name a few, helps students develop 21st-century skills by giving them real-world, hands-on experiences. Finally, as the world continues to be transformed by technology, employers are looking for skilled workers to meet their requirements in today's digital tools and platforms.

Creating online content helps students to become good digital citizens. Digital citizenship is difficult to define because it means different things to different people. Still, according to Matthew Lynch of EducationWeek, digital citizenship is merely using technology responsibly and ethically. Using technology responsibly implies that users are thoughtful and intentional in their online activity. In other words, students should follow the cyber Golden Rule "treat other users how they want to be treated."

TEACHING STRATEGY:

Teach students to THINK before posting online. They should ask themselves the following questions, T = Is it true? H = Is it helpful? I = Is it inspiring? N = Is it necessary? And K = Is it kind? Following this advice could significantly reduce incidences of cyberbullying and other malicious acts perpetrated online.

Another way to think about responsibly using technology is to conduct oneself online the same way one would in real life. In other words, users should never say or do anything online that they wouldn't say or do in front of their own families. In addition, digital citizens must be ethical. This means that they should never appropriate anything from the web that they do not have a legal right to possess. Students must give proper attributions to all materials that were created and produced by someone else. Students should also understand the rules related to the public domain, copyright, trademark, patent laws, and the creative commons and royalty-free media.

1.6 Career & Life Skills to Be Successful in the 21st Century

Over 2,500 years ago, the Greek philosopher Heraclitus of Ephesus famously said, "Change is the only constant in life." His words ring truer today than ever before in history due to the significant role tech has played in changing the world around us. According to Career Change statistics, the average person will change careers five to seven times during their working life, and 30 percent of the workforce will change careers or jobs every year. The fluidity in career change is due in part to rapid growth in the various tech-related industries. A recent Gallop report on the millennial generation revealed that between 1981 and 1996, 21 percent of millennials changed jobs within the past year. This is over three times the number of non-millennials who were queried at the same time.

Further, by the time today's students reach the age of forty-two, it is predicted that they will have had approximately ten different jobs. There are several reasons why young people change jobs so often. These workers do not feel the stigma of frequent job-hopping, as older generations do, and will leave their current employer for higher wages, to develop their skills, put their career on the fast track, and find a better fit in terms of work culture and values. The old notion of an employee spending forty years with a company and retiring with a pension and a gold watch is quickly becoming an anachronism in the modern world. For these reasons, adaptability and flexibility are critically important for today's students to be successful.

Businesses and organizations have become flatter, nimbler, and more flexible to stay competitive in the modern world. As a result, today's workforce needs to be adaptable and flexible too. Unlike past jobs, which were relatively immutable, workers must be able to rapidly adjust to meet today's exigencies on a real-time basis. Workers need to be open to new ideas and ways of doing things. They must be able to work independently or as members of teams as work requires. They must be able to juggle multiple tasks simultaneously and not get flustered when conditions quickly change. Phrases like "that's not my job," "that's not the way we used to do it," "no one ever told/showed me how" have no place in the modern workplace. One's ability to adapt to new circumstances by taking the initiative to solve problems quickly and efficiently allows for greater flexibility, resulting in more significant career opportunities.

Employers are looking for individuals who will take responsibility for their work and will assume leadership roles in the workplace. Leadership may be formal, such as holding a particular job title that wields authority and power over others. Or it may be informal, such as when employees choose to follow an individual because they respect and trust them. Either way, influential leaders take the initiative to get a project done rather than waiting around to be told what to do. Additionally, leaders build confidence in their teams and help to create and maintain positive work environments. As Mark Twain once wrote, "Keep away from people who try to belittle your ambitions. Small people always do that, but the great make you feel that you, too, can become great." In other words, leadership is about taking the necessary actions to bring out the best in the people around you. It is about putting others before yourself. Influential leaders maintain a high degree of positivity and try to see the good in the bad. As the famous saying goes, "You may not be able to control every situation and its outcome, but you can control your attitude and how you deal with it." Nothing is as certain as change, and influential leaders can adapt to it even when the change creates uncertainty.

The think tank Institute for the Future, named cross-cultural competency as one of the ten most essential skills for the modern workforce. We live in a globally connected world, which puts a premium on diversity and adaptability. This is mainly because innovation stems from diverse people's collaborative efforts, bringing different perspectives, ideologies, and experiences to the table. Social scientist Adam Galinsky points out that people who develop strong relationships with someone from another country and culture become more creative and do better on creativity tests. And as has already been discussed, creativity and innovation are the keys to future success. As beneficial as cross-cultural collaboration can be, it can have negative consequences if one is not prepared to engage with others from different backgrounds. Diversity promotes innovation and creativity, which are good things. However, it can also create misunderstanding through a lack of cultural awareness and ineffective communication. To bridge cultural barriers, students must be able to empathize with people who are different from themselves. They must effectively communicate their perspective to others who may not share their value system or worldview. This is more often than not achieved through active and empathetic listening. They should be able to integrate diverse perspectives to create new solutions for problems. Finally, cross-cultural competency means being able to resolve conflict in productive ways that do not damage relationships. It is essential to recognize that solving problems is not a zero-sum game. It is not about winning or losing. Instead, it is about compromise and empowerment, finding solutions that appeal to all involved.

Social awareness is the ability to take the perspective of others from diverse backgrounds and cultures. One of the most effective ways to do this is by developing empathy for people who are different. According to the Merriam-Webster dictionary, empathy is defined as "the action of understanding, being aware of, being sensitive to, and vicariously experiencing the feelings, thoughts, and experience of another of either the past or present without having the feelings, thoughts, and experience fully communicated in an objectively explicit manner." In other words, empathetic people try to step into the shoes of others and to try to understand them on a deep and visceral level. There are several ways to develop an empathetic understanding. Perhaps the most powerful, however, is through active listening. Active listening means focusing on the speaker and understanding what the other person is saying without making assumptions based on personal experience. By slowing down and concentrating on what the speaker is saying to include the message's emotions, one can provide support, not just sympathy. However, it is impossible to fully understand someone else's lived experience because we are all spectacularly unique. But an honest and sincere attempt should be made to appreciate their perspective. Social awareness takes effort, but all students must develop this vital skill as social awareness helps build positive relationships, productivity, and an overall positive environment built on trust and mutual respect. Curiosity and a genuine desire to learn more about diverse cultures are vital to becoming socially aware. To learn more about other cultures, have open and honest conversations with diverse friends and colleagues. Read assorted authors concerning subjects of race, ethnicity, culture, gender, and history. Other ways include visiting cultural institutions in the community, such as museums and various minority-owned businesses. Watch movies and television shows that reflect diverse perspectives and characters. Listen to podcasts and vlogs that present alternative views.

1.7 Questions for Reflection

1. Describe the knowledge, skills, and dispositions that students will need to be successful in the 21st-century, technology rich economy. What are some methods for teaching these?

2. What are some examples of 21st-century skills? Why are they important? And how can educators teach them?

3. If project-based learning is an effective way to teach students 21st-century skills and prepare them for the knowledge economy, why is PBL not used more in school?

4. Why is digital literacy a vital skill for the knowledge economy? What are some strategies for teaching students digital literacy?

CHAPTER

02

Effective Teaching for the 21st Century

This is the value of the teacher, who looks at a face and says there's something behind that and I want to reach that person, I want to influence that person, I want to encourage that person, I want to enrich, I want to call out that person who is behind that face, behind that color, behind that language, behind that tradition, behind that culture. I believe you can do it. I know what was done for me.

—MAYA ANGELOU

Were all instructors to realize that the quality of mental process, not the production of correct answers, is the measure of educative growth something hardly less than a revolution in teaching would be worked.

—JOHN DEWEY, *DEMOCRACY AND EDUCATION*

Teachers matter! In fact, research suggests that the most important controllable factor for increasing student achievement at school is the quality of the teacher. Studies in both Tennessee and Texas revealed that students who had effective teachers significantly outperformed those who did not. And when students had effective teachers three years in a row, they scored up to fifty percentage points higher on mathematics tests than students who had ineffective teachers (Sanders & Rivers, 1996). In addition, the National Bureau of Economic Research published a longitudinal study of over a million students that pointed out learners who were taught by highly effective teachers had significantly better long-term outcomes than those who were not. These students were more likely to attend college, earn higher lifetime salaries, and were less likely to have children while in adolescence. The same study demonstrated that by replacing a teacher at the bottom 5 percent with a teacher of average effectiveness, that teacher could increase a student's lifetime income by approximately $250,000 per classroom (Chetty, Friedman, & Rockoff, 2013). As leading education expert Dr. Robert Marzano points out, "The one single factor that surfaced as the single most influential component of an effective school is the individual teachers within that school."

President George W. Bush's signature education law, the No Child Left Behind Act (NCLB) of 2001, required all teachers who taught a core subject, English language learners, and students with disabilities to be "highly qualified." In trying to ensure that an excellent teacher taught every student, the law set minimum requirements for effectiveness, including having a bachelor's degree, state certification, and demonstrating competency in the subjects taught. Unfortunately, there was little evidence that NCLB resulted in significant student achievement and was replaced by the Every Student Succeeds Act in 2015, repealing the highly qualified teacher requirements. The two laws exemplify the conversation about what constitutes an effective teacher. The former explicitly outlines highly qualified teacher status elements, while the latter refrains from being prescriptive about how states should address the question. Common questions about teacher effectiveness include do degrees and credentials make teachers successful? Are experienced teachers more effective than new teachers? Do student results on high-stakes tests identify teaching effectiveness? Can administrative observations and performance reviews accurately determine how effective a teacher is and make teachers better? Perhaps effective teaching is beyond classification and quantification and is best identified by experienced educators who "know it when they see it."

It may be difficult to pinpoint precisely what effective teaching is. Still, according to the International Handbook of Research on Teachers and Teaching (2009), effective teaching can be thought of in terms of the teacher's behaviors, such as warmth, civility, and clarity, teacher's beliefs about their students, and the teacher's knowledge of their profession as evidenced by improvements in student achievement. Therefore, this chapter will focus on the professional knowledge that all teachers need to know to be highly effective educators.

Objectives:

- ➲ Describe teachers' professional knowledge of best teaching practices such as using students' prior knowledge, how students organize their knowledge and how to motivate students to learn.

- ➲ Explain why educators must have a strong grasp of content knowledge, content pedagogical knowledge, and curriculum knowledge to be effective.

- ➲ Describe why mastery learning is important and the various components of mastery learning to include scaffolding, voice and choice, practice, and feedback.

2.1 Teachers' Professional Knowledge of Their Craft

At the core of effective teaching is the teacher's professional knowledge. According to research, there are three main areas that teachers must be highly knowledgeable in to be effective teachers. They are content knowledge, pedagogical knowledge, and teachers' knowledge of their students and families. Think of each area of professional knowledge as one of three legs on a stool. If one leg is missing or underdeveloped, the stool will topple over, or at the very least, be off-balance. Anecdotally, it takes five to six years of teaching experience before teachers reach high levels of effectiveness, as each competency must be developed thoroughly and proportionally. Some teachers will come into the profession with excellent content knowledge while lacking in pedagogical skills. These educators usually take a "teacher-centered" approach and make great lecturers but have difficulty effectively transmitting their expertise to students or providing adequate learning opportunities. This is why it is sometimes challenging for people to change careers and become teachers. Even though they may have been highly competent and knowledgeable individuals in their previous vocations, they will not be effective teachers if they lack pedagogical expertise and relational skills. Other teachers may be well versed in the latest teaching approaches and develop excellent relationships with students but are weak in content knowledge. This is one of the criticisms of schools of education because they usually emphasize pedagogy over the content, unbalancing the stool in favor of teaching and sidelining content.

Be deliberate about your professional learning. I knew early on in my teaching career, as a high school U.S. history teacher, that I wanted to become the best educator that I could be. I knew that it would be essential to master both content and pedagogy, and I believed I could do that by attaining advanced degrees. When I entered the classroom, I had already earned a bachelor's degree in U.S. history and a master's degree in education through an alternative route to licensure (ARL) program. I felt the formal education I received had prepared me well in my content area and professional teaching knowledge. After a few years, however, I went back to school to earn a master's degree in U.S. history. I did this because I love learning, and I wanted the challenge. Earning an advanced degree in history requires critical thinking, analysis, research, and writing skills. I am glad that I did because earning the degree gave me the confidence to teach my students effectively. Additionally, the degree opened new doors of professional possibility as it qualified me to teach U.S. history at the collegiate level. After focusing on my content knowledge for many years, I wanted to hone my pedagogical skills and expand my influence and expertise. I did this by becoming a National Board Certified Teacher. National Board Certification (NBC) is an advanced teaching credential offered by the National Board for Professional Teaching Standards (NBPTS). The certification requires teachers to become reflective practitioners by demonstrating the expertise of student learning through the mastery of NBPTS standards and subject content knowledge. The last piece of my formal professional learning was earning an educational doctorate in curriculum, instruction, and assessment. This was an opportunity to synthesize my professional learning by creating an original work of scholarship. I wanted to share my professional journey to demonstrate the deliberate steps I took to master content and pedagogy. I am not suggesting that my path is the only one or that all teachers need to earn advanced degrees. With new forms of professional learning such as micro-credentials, MOOCS, and video blogs, to name a few, teachers have many choices about how they grow as professional educators. The point is to be deliberate. Think about your areas of strengths and weaknesses, and work passionately to balance the stool.

2.2 Best Teaching Practices

Pedagogy, in its simplest terms, is the science, art, and craft of teaching. Teaching is a science because there is a body of research-based knowledge and practices that have been proven to be effective in educating students. Through advancements in understanding cognitive, motivational, and developmental psychology, organizational and group learning, and diversity studies, educators can maximize the learning process to elicit student academic achievement for all learners. It is an art because of the myriad creative ways a teacher can go about educating their students. The innovative approaches, methods, and techniques are reminiscent of a painter's choices about their craft, such as what brushes to use, color palette, and subject of their painting. The teacher, like the artist, may not always be able to tell you exactly what technique they are using or explain their approach technically. Still, the result is a beautiful piece of art arrived at by experience through the process of trial and error. Finally, teaching is a craft because it is based on a set of abilities that are learned over time. Freshly minted teachers from educator preparation programs are beginning a very long journey of self-discovery and transformation. To become master teachers, they must engage in consistent reflection, continued study, and persistent practice. They must arrive at their teaching philosophy through their personal life's journey and tap into their unique passions, talents, and skills.

There is no "one-size-fits-all" magic bullet in teaching, and teachers must find the approaches and strategies that work best for them and their students, often through trial and error. In addition to research-based best practices, effective teachers make the human connections and relationships necessary for effective learning.

2.3   What Students Already Know

The first principle of effective teaching is for the teacher to tap into students' prior knowledge. Student learning should be built upon what they already know about a particular topic. Students acquire their knowledge both formally and informally. Educators often emphasize things learned formally in school without fully appreciating the knowledge, skills, and dispositions students bring from beyond the schoolhouse doors. Teachers can maximize student learning by understanding and incorporating students' lived experiences to include attitudes and beliefs into their lessons. Understanding students' prior knowledge will help teachers recognize students' gaps in understanding and their misconceptions. Teachers must address students' prior knowledge early in their learning because their experience, or lack thereof, can either hinder or help in the learning process.

TEACHING STRATEGY:

There are several ways in which teachers can activate students' prior knowledge. One of the most enduring is utilizing the KWL graphic organizer. In this exercise, students create a three-column graphic organizer (or use premade KWL graphic organizer). Students brainstorm everything they know or think they know about a given topic in the first column. I tell students to write down everything no matter how "off-topic." Everything is fair game: movies, T.V. shows, books, music, video games, trips to historical sites, or museums. When students realize that their response does not have to be "academic," they tend to open up and provide much more information. The second column is what students want to know about the topic. Again, I like to stress that there is no "correct" answer. Their curiosity and desire to know things are deeply personal, and I like to point out that learning is a voyage of self-discovery. The more you learn, the more you realize how much you do not know. The third column is what students have learned after the lesson is completed. Using this approach is an excellent way for students to engage in "metacognition" or thinking about their learning.

2.4 How Students Organize their Knowledge

How students organize their knowledge is also essential. Research suggests that students must link new learning to prior knowledge in long-term memory to learn new things. This process creates concepts developed from experience, reasoning, and imagination. Persons with expert knowledge of a subject have networks of concepts connected in various meaningful ways around their field's integral principles. New learners do not have these deep connections yet, as their prior learning may be fragmented and incomplete. However, due to neuroplasticity, our brains can form new neural connections over time. In other words, our brains are adaptive and can grow in response to new learning.

TEACHING STRATEGY:

Teachers can help students build concepts through a process called concept mapping. A concept map is a visual organization and representation of knowledge. Examples of concept maps include flowcharts, spider maps, hierarchical maps, and systems maps. Concept maps can be used throughout a lesson to help students connect prior learning to new ideas and concepts. They help educators "see" their students' thought processes and how they understand the content. Concept maps have several applications. First, they can be used to brainstorm at the beginning of a unit of study or as a preassessment to see what students already know about a topic. Second, they can be used in small group activities by assigning a concept or idea to each group to analyze and synthesize information. Third, they can be used in whole-class instruction to create a springboard from which to discuss relationships between various concepts in a unit of study. Fourth, concept maps are excellent ways for students to organize their research or ideas for writing projects or other types of investigative learning. Finally, concept maps can also be used for reflection and metacognition at the end of a unit of study, helping students see connections between concepts and the unit's "big picture." Research indicates that using concept maps has several benefits, including assisting visual learners to see interrelated concepts and the "big picture," memory recall, transferability of concepts, and applications from one subject to another (Ellis, Rudnitsky, & Silverstein, 2004).

2.5 Student Motivation

Motivation is an integral component of learning. Intrinsically motivated students have an internal desire to succeed and learn more because they are personally interested and invested in learning. They derive a sense of personal accomplishment and satisfaction from their learning. Intrinsic motivation is the opposite of extrinsic motivation. Extrinsic motivation is when student performance is tied to an external reward or punishment, such as grades. A study performed at Princeton University indicated that intrinsic motivation is a much more powerful motivator of student performance and even goes so far as to point out that external motivation may be damaging, suggesting "external incentives are weak reinforcers in the short run, and negative reinforcers in the long run" (Benabou & Tirole, 2003). Motivated learners demonstrate perseverance and grit and do not give up easily when faced with adversity and setbacks. Research suggests that teachers can motivate their students by cultivating meaningful and respectful relationships and developing a growth mindset based on high expectations and clearly defined goals. Studies indicate that teachers' high expectations of their students result in student achievement. One of the most influential is the Pygmalion in the Classroom (1968) study. In this investigation, a Harvard professor and an elementary school principal told elementary school teachers that a recent standardized test revealed that some students were academic "late bloomers" who would be experiencing extraordinary academic growth in the coming school year. Several students were selected at random to be the high-growth students when in actuality, the standardized test was never given. The study found that because teachers believed that certain students would be high achievers, their expectations for those students changed, resulting in student achievement. In other words, when teachers expected their students to perform well, they usually did.

Thirty years ago, Dr. Carol Dweck, in her influential book *Mindset: The New Psychology of Success*, postulated that students could develop a growth mindset. That is the belief that learning and intelligence can grow with hard work and determination. Dweck points out, "In a growth mindset, people believe that their most basic abilities can be developed through dedication and hard work—brains and talent are just the starting point. This view creates a love of learning and a resilience that is essential for great accomplishment." Students with a growth mindset embrace challenges, persist in the face of setbacks, see effort as the path to mastery, learn from criticism, and find inspiration in others' success. Unfortunately, many students and teachers stubbornly cling to the notion of a fixed mindset in which intelligence, talent, and creativity are static and immutable. As a result, these students seldom stray outside of their comfort zones and push themselves to be the best they can be. When teachers fail to cultivate a growth mindset in their students, they rob them of their unrealized potential to do great things.

Daniel Pink, the author of *Drive: The Surprising Truth About What Motivates Us*, points out that much of what we know about motivation is wrong. Traditional approaches to managing behavior such as rewards and punishments are anachronistic in modern times because today's students and workers must possess 21st-century skills such as creativity, collaboration, and problem-solving. The carrot and the stick approach may be appropriate when the task is algorithmic, reinforcing basic mechanical skills. Still, it is less effective at motivating people to do creative work and other higher-order thinking tasks. Pink points out that "The science shows that the secret to high performance isn't our biological drive or our reward-and-punishment drive, but how our third drive—our deep-seated desire to direct our own lives, to extend and expand our abilities, and to make a contribution" is what truly inspires us. To motivate people beyond doing simple tasks, Pink suggests that workers should be supported in the three areas of autonomy, mastery, and purpose. Autonomy means that people have a voice and choice in their work and increases engagement versus simple compliance. Mastery means that people desire to get better at what they do and learn new skills. Finally, purpose implies that people have an innate desire to do something that has meaning and is important to them. According to William Damon, the author of *The Path to Purpose: How Young People Find Their Calling*, purpose is a "stable and generalized intention to accomplish something that is at the same time meaningful to the self and consequential for the world beyond the self" (Damon, 2010, p. 33). For example, students want to know why they are doing a particular task at school. They want to see how the assignment relates to them and why they must do it. But to understand our student's sense of purpose, it is essential to understand who our students are.

Most students today belong to Generation Z. Gen Z is comprised of people born between the years 1997 and 2012 and are between the ages of six and twenty-four. There are 72 million members of Gen Z in the United States and over 2 billion globally. It is the second-largest generation in American history after the millennials, which consists of 72.26 million. Gen Z is also the most diverse generation in the nation's history, as 48 percent report being non-Caucasian. Further, diversity matters to them across several dimensions, including race and gender. A recent survey by the job recruiting website Monster indicated that 83 percent of Gen Z job candidates said that a prospective employers' commitment to diversity and inclusion is essential in their decision to work for them.

Just as the Great Depression and WWII shaped the Greatest Generations' worldview, and 9/11 and the global economic crisis in 2007 influenced the millennial generation, events have influenced Gen Z in significant ways. They have had to contend with extreme political polarization, the racial reckoning stemming from the murder of George Floyd and other unarmed Black people at the hands of the police, and the deadly worldwide coronavirus pandemic. The subsequent quarantine ripped students from their schools, social groups, sporting activities, and just about every aspect of "normal life," causing severe emotional trauma for many students. A recent study indicated that 71 percent of students reported feelings of isolation, anxiety, and depression as they experienced fear and worry over their health and the health of loved ones.

Despite these incredible challenges, Gen Z is on track to be the best-educated cohort in American history. According to the Pew Research Center, 57 percent of eighteen-to-twenty-one-year-olds who are no longer in high school were enrolled in a two- or four-year college. That is significantly higher than millennials, with 52 percent going to college in 2003 and 43 percent of Gen X going to college in 1987. Gen Zers were born into a high-tech world of high-speed Internet and mobile technology and are sometimes referred to as digital natives or the iGeneration. To illustrate this point, 95 percent of thirteen-to-seventeen-year-olds reported that they have access to a smartphone and use on average up to five screens a day, spending ten hours or more on electronic devices. Gen Z came of age at a time when they had instant access to news and information from around the world instantaneously, connecting them in ways that were unimaginable by previous generations. Despite the significant amount of time spent on devices, however, Gen Z craves real-life connections that go beyond computer screens.

Gen Z is significantly impacting the workplace. Demographers predict that by 2025, Gen Z will be 30 percent of the U.S. workforce. That percentage will continue to grow as the generation matures and moves through school and higher education. While wages and working conditions are significant issues for most Gen Z, they are also interested in making a difference. According to a report from Wespire, Gen Z has a "dream big" and "we can change the world" attitude. They are the first generation to prioritize purpose over money and are referred to by many as the "change generation." They want to see a connection between what they are doing at work and broader social impacts. Meaningful work drives motivation, as 75 percent believe that work should have a greater meaning than just a paycheck. They want work that matters that is positive and purposeful. This attitude is reflected in the companies that have adopted positive social missions as part of their corporate identities. Take, for example, a recent social media advertisement from HP: "The world needs our actions now. It's why HP is taking bold steps to drive climate action, protect human rights, and accelerate digital equity. #SustainableImpact.

Educators can connect to and support Gen Z by helping them explore their purpose. Research suggests that when students have a sense of purpose, they have higher engagement, they approach their studies more efficiently, and they experience higher degrees of success and satisfaction in their studies (Xerri, Radford, & Shacklock, 2018). There are several things that teachers can do to help students discover and nurture their purpose at school.

CULTIVATE CURIOSITY

Classrooms should be places where students explore their worlds to include the people, ideas, events, and controversies that have shaped them. Give students opportunities to cultivate their curiosity by creating opportunities to investigate personally interesting topics. When students find something that ignites their passion, teachers should encourage them to explore it further. Sometimes students need to be encouraged that what they care about matters, even if it is not academically related. Too often, we elevate testable material over everything else, including the things students care about most. We must validate our students' curiosity and interests to help them find their purpose. Pedagogical approaches that cultivate curiosity include project-based learning and inquiry-based learning, or any method that allows students to ask questions and explore personal interests. Additionally, students should be taught to be skeptical. Derived from the Greek word *skeptikos*, "to inquire," skeptics require evidence before accepting a premise to be true. Teach students to challenge the status quo and conventional wisdom by developing an open mind and the ability to ask good questions.

SELF-REFLECTION

Students should have regular opportunities to reflect on their purpose by thinking about their life's journey. Have students contemplate the challenges they have had to overcome, their successes, and what brings them genuine joy. Students should be aware that the process of acquiring a goal and fulfilling their purpose is just as important as the destination. Finally, students should think about how much time, energy, and effort they are willing to invest to achieve their purpose. A thoughtful cost and benefit analysis can help students realize what is truly important in their lives and the sacrifices required to achieve their goals. Teachers can get students to reflect through reflective thinking activities such as a think-pair-share, class and small group discussion prompts, journaling, and exit tickets.

GOAL SETTING

Teachers can help students set goals by assisting them in articulating clear and measurable areas of improvement. The goal may be academic, personal, professional, or a combination of all three. An excellent way to introduce goalsetting is by having students set SMART goals. A SMART goal is specific. Students must address a specific thing that they want to achieve or improve upon. The more detailed, the better, encourage students to articulate what they want to accomplish by writing a clear goal statement. Second, the goal must be measurable, which means that students need to have a way to gauge their progress to know if they are on the right track or if they need to adjust their strategy. Third, the goals must be attainable. In other words, there must be a reasonable expectation that the goal can be accomplished within a certain amount of time. Fourth, the goal must be relevant, meaning that the goal should be directed toward a long-term objective. Finally, the goal needs to be time-based. This means that the goal needs to be accomplished within a realistic but ambitious time frame to motivate students to prioritize and achieve their goals.

▌ MODEL AND MENTOR

Teachers should model for their students what living with a sense of purpose looks like. They can do this by sharing how their values, worldview, and goals influenced their purpose and their steps to live out their purpose in their daily lives. Students should understand that finding one's purpose is not something everyone discovers right away, but it will eventually become clear with persistence, determination, and time. Teachers can mentor students as they search for their purpose through open dialogue about what matters most to them. Teachers can support their students through the process of self-discovery by being good listeners and cultivating respectful and healthy relationships.

▌ CONNECT TO THE REAL WORLD

Too often, students see school as a set of perfunctory "hoops" that they must jump through to graduate and begin their "real lives." Instead, teachers should make school relevant by connecting what students learn with the world beyond the schoolhouse gate. Teachers can provide students with opportunities to examine issues rooted in the real world by introducing the news, events, people, and controversies that matter to them.

2.6 Content Knowledge

There is an ongoing debate within education circles about the appropriate place of content knowledge in the curriculum. Those who take a more progressive position contend that content knowledge should not be the primary educational outcome. Instead, students should be engaged in learning and applying the 21st-century skills of critical thinking, communication, collaboration, and creativity. Educators who hold this view argue that schools need to produce students who are flexible thinkers and who can adapt to their quickly changing world, not be weighted down with unnecessary "facts." Further, what information is required can be quickly "Googled" using smartphone or computer technology, freeing the student to engage in more worthwhile endeavors besides "memorization and regurgitation." The other, more traditional point of view argues that schools should focus on teaching students content. They believe that our society has a defined body of knowledge that must be passed on from generation to generation. For example, author and educational thinker E. D. Hirsch points out, "all human communities are found upon specific shared information," that to fully participate in contemporary society, one must be familiar with the background information of which most writers and speakers assume their audience possesses. In other words, citizens must not only be able to read and write, but they must also have cultural literacy if they are to become fully participating members of society. According to this view, schools should play an integral role in transferring this knowledge from older generations to newer ones. In addition, teaching content knowledge is integral to the process of acculturation or assimilation of the dominant culture. In this view, teachers help students develop and understand American history, democratic institutions, language, and traditions to build a cohesive civil body politic.

The Merriam-Webster dictionary defines teaching as "to cause to know something." And as the adage goes, "you can't teach what you don't know." That is why content knowledge is essential, especially in the upper grades, where content becomes more specific and specialized, requiring a deep understanding of the discipline being taught. According to the National Research Council, "Teachers' capacity to pose questions, select tasks, evaluate their pupil's understanding, and to make curricular decisions all depend on how they understand the subject matter." Further, research indicates that teachers with solid knowledge of their subjects yield more significant student academic outcomes than teachers without in-depth content knowledge (Baumert, Jürgen & Kunter, & Mareike 2013). Research indicates that content knowledge is essential for good reading comprehension. This is because good readers go beyond the decoding of individual words when they read. The more content-specific knowledge the student has, the better they will read, and the better they read, the more they will learn. As cognitive scientist Daniel T. Willingham explains:

> Research shows that reading depends on a broad knowledge of all subjects: history, science, mathematics, literature, drama, music, and so on. Furthermore, it makes sense that subject matter knowledge is sequenced. It's commonly appreciated that mathematical concepts build on one another, and they are easier to learn if they are sequenced properly. The same is true of other subjects. It's easier to understand why the last remnants of European colonialism crumbled in the 1950s if you know something about World War II. It's easier to understand World War II if you know something about the Great Depression. And so on. So the content that students will learn in the earliest grades is hugely important. It's the bedrock of everything that is to come (Willingham, 2015, p. 102–103).

Albert Einstein said that "creativity is more important than knowledge." And as we have seen, the 21st-century skill of creativity and outside-of-the-box thinking are the new currency of the knowledge economy. But as psychologist Robert Sternberg points out, "one cannot apply what one knows in a practical manner if one does not know anything to apply." In other words, content knowledge is not a zero-sum game in which it is all one thing or another. Instead, teachers should balance critical content knowledge with the skills and dispositions to extend their thinking beyond the simple recall of facts and apply, analyze, connect, create, critique, synthesize and evaluate what they have learned. As education author and executive director of No More Marking, Daisy Christodoulou, points out, "If we fail to teach knowledge, we fail to learn" and "factual knowledge is closely integrated with creativity, problem-solving and analysis. It allows these skills to happen." The key is to find the right balance. This is why teaching is a craft because it takes time, reflection, and experience to know when students have mastered enough content to move on to more intellectually stimulating work. But to be clear, both are necessary to an effective 21st-century education.

2.7 Content Pedagogical Knowledge

Besides having solid content knowledge and general pedagogical knowledge, educational psychologist Lee Shulman (1986) postulates that content pedagogical knowledge, or CPK, is the third major component of teaching expertise. CPK is the intersection of what teachers know about their subjects and students and their general understanding of teaching. It is specialized knowledge unique to teachers that makes them effective at teaching. For example, science teachers are different than scientists, not because they lack subject matter knowledge. But science teachers organize their knowledge from a teaching perspective, and it is used to help students learn specific concepts. On the other hand, scientists organize their knowledge from a research perspective that is used to conduct research to develop knowledge in the field. As Aristotle famously put it, "Those that know do, those that understand teach." Research indicates that teachers who possess high levels of CPK have higher levels of curricular and developmental outcomes (Gudmundsdottir, 1987a, b). Additionally, high levels of CPK have been linked to students' enjoyment and engagement in learning and better student feedback (Creasy, Whipp, & Jackson, 2012). According to Shulman (1986), CPK

> ... embodies the aspects of content most germane to its teachability. Within the category of pedagogical content knowledge I include, for the most regularly taught topics in one's subject area, the most useful forms of representation of those ideas, the most powerful analogies, illustrations, examples, explanations, and demonstrations—in a word, the ways of representing and formulating the subject that make it comprehensible to others ... [It] also includes an understanding of what makes the learning of specific concepts easy or difficult: the conceptions and preconceptions that students of different ages and backgrounds bring with them to the learning (p. 9).

Sometimes CPK is referred to as craft knowledge. This is because CPK takes time to develop and hone through a period of trial and error and deep reflection. Through this process, teachers arrive at works and what doesn't based on experience. They understand how essential concepts, skills, and knowledge are organized and can be taught to students to elicit academic achievement for all learners. They know that students can best understand the complexities of specific topics by using various pedagogical approaches.

TEACHING STRATEGY:

In a U.S. history course, teachers demonstrate CPK when they teach students what "doing" history involves and how we "know" what happened in the past. In other words, they are teaching the discipline's epistemology or studying the origin, nature, limits, and methods of knowledge. According to research, teachers must recognize students' understanding of the subject, then determine teaching materials, content organization, and learning activities that represent the discipline. Representations in history include knowledge of the past and how historians conduct their professional work to include their historical thinking or historical thinking habits. Teachers with strong CPK use their students' disciplinary and subject knowledge to advance their understanding of history beyond memorizing names, dates, and places (Monte-Sano & Budano, 2013). An excellent way to teach students these habits of mind is to utilize the document-based question or DBQ. A DBQ is a type of essay in which students think like historians by employing their skills of identifying causation, patterns of continuity and change, argumentation based on their knowledge of history, and appropriate use of relevant evidence. Students must be able to interpret and synthesize various primary and secondary source evidence pertaining to the historical event in question. The source material usually consists of differing or conflicting points of view. For example, in a unit about the American Revolution, a writing prompt may ask students to compare and contrast the arguments for and against the colonists declaring their independence from England. Documents provided could include a speech from a member of parliament, a letter written by George Washington, Felix's Petition, the Stamp Act, and the Declaration of Independence. DBQs go beyond simple factual recall and require students to:

➲ Write a strong thesis that can be proven true using the documents and the student's knowledge of history.

➲ Determine the strengths and weaknesses of source evidence by analyzing the author's point of view, purpose, audience, and context of the evidence.

➲ Demonstrate the ability to make connections between the documents. For example, to identify corroboration of evidence and when evidence conflicts with one another.

Highly effective teachers use their CPK to push their students to become independent critical thinkers. They see the big picture and possess the flexibility to choose the teaching method that does justice to the topic. Other approaches may include engaging students in debates concerning an enduring historical problem, such as the pros and cons of representative government, the perennial issue of growing wealth inequality, or mass incarceration. Or teachers could conduct a Socratic seminar to investigate the role of social media in civic life. In other words, the teachers' effective use of CPK is instrumental to effective teaching for the 21st century.

2.8 Curriculum Knowledge

There is much confusion regarding the differences between standards and curriculum. Educational standards are the learning goals for what students should know and be able to do. As used by most teachers, the word *curriculum* describes the academic content, experiences, and teaching materials that make up the totality of students learning. In other words, standards are what is to be learned, and the curriculum is what is taught. There are several aspects of the curriculum that directly and indirectly impact student learning. They are the recommended, written, supported, tested, taught, and learned curriculum. The recommended curriculum is a curriculum produced by experts in their fields and is usually published by professional organizations. For example, the National Council for the Social Studies has published standards that help guide states and districts in crafting curriculum documents at the local levels. The written curriculum consolidates documents produced by the state and school districts that indicate what is taught. This is usually in the form of curriculum guides and scope and sequence documents. Unfortunately, many state and local curriculum standards reflect the cultural majority's ideological and political vantage points that produced them. This position routinely excludes women, racial, and religious minorities (Wills, 2019).

The supported curriculum is indicated by the availability of instructional materials, such as textbooks, technology, and manipulatives. Research suggests that teachers use the textbook between 70 and 95 percent for all classroom instruction (Gay, 2010). That number is likely lower today due to the proliferation of web-based resources but still illustrates the degree to which teachers rely on the text to drive instruction. Teachers should be aware that textbooks are "cultural artifacts" that reflect the dominant group's hegemony by portraying "politically approved knowledge." In other words, textbooks continue to mitigate the roles of diverse actors. For example, when people of color are introduced, it is generally a bland, conservative, conformist, and "safe" way emphasizing racial harmony rather than examining unpleasant and uncomfortable history (Gay, 2010). Many teachers lament that they would include more diverse voices if they had the resources to do so. A lack of high-quality curriculum materials is a significant impediment to introducing a culturally responsive curriculum. Continued budget cuts to education across the country will likely exacerbate the problem.

The tested curriculum is the information that is assessed on state, district, and teacher prepared tests. Due to perennial shortages of teacher and student facetime, it is not taught if it is not tested. As a result, the curriculum is significantly narrowed, squeezing out diverse voices making room for test preparation of testable material only. The taught curriculum is what teachers do in the classroom, which can sometimes look different from what is published in state and local standards and curriculum documents. The most crucial curriculum, however, is the learned curriculum. The learned curriculum is what students leave the classroom knowing as a result of what was taught. Two other forms of the curriculum are not visible in school curriculum documents but profoundly impact diverse learners. They are the hidden curriculum and the excluded curriculum.

The hidden curriculum refers to what students learn as a result of the school's culture and climate. It is not intentionally taught but based on students' perceptions of their school's priorities and objectives. For example, a school may claim to be a welcoming place for diverse learners. But upon a closer look, little is done by the school community to include students and their families in school activities, organizations, and events. How teachers prioritize time and resources are two components of the hidden curriculum. Teachers can never have enough time, and the way teachers allocate it speaks volumes about their priorities. Making time in the curriculum for diverse voices and points of view should be a priority for all teachers and requires them to make a conscious decision to include them. Teaching materials with diverse points of view should be incorporated into the curriculum whenever it is appropriate to do so. A culturally responsive approach to the curriculum means that diverse voices are interwoven into the lesson and not just "add-ons."

The excluded curriculum is what has been left out. This may occur unintentionally and be the result of a teacher's lack of knowledge. Or the teacher may intentionally leave out content because they may wish to avoid controversy. Exclusion of controversial topics frequently happens in biology classes, for example, when teachers skip over teaching the theory of evolution for fear of offending conservatively religious students and their families. The excluded curriculum can be found in U.S. history courses as well. James Loewen, author of the best-selling book *Lies My Teacher Told Me*, argues that U.S. history has been "whitewashed" in public schools. Meaning that publishers have intentionally removed sensitive or controversial material to sell as many textbooks as possible. This is especially true regarding states that purchase large numbers of books, such as Texas and California. Loewen points out:

- Despite their accomplishments, George Washington and Thomas Jefferson were not perfect men and made their fortunes primarily on the backs of enslaved people.

- The Civil War was fought precisely over slavery and not "states' rights" or anything else.

- Abraham Lincoln did not believe that Black people were equal to White people and wanted to send them back to Africa.

➲ In the century following the Civil War, the thousands of lynchings of African American men and women were often occasions for picnics by White people. Some even received body parts as souvenirs.

➲ White people were responsible for genocide against Indigenous peoples, and our leaders established boarding schools to try to "civilize" Indigenous children by destroying their culture.

➲ Several progressive New Deal programs (e.g., Social Security and the G.I. Bill) intentionally discriminated against African Americans.

Those who hold traditional views of America as an exceptional nation claim that teaching America's past, faults and all, is little more than "revisionist" history. Teachers should spend less time focusing on America's mistakes and more time reveling in its exceptionalism. The history versus heritage argument is not going away anytime soon. The truth is that teachers have tremendous amounts of content to cover and little time to do it. For every person, event, or concept taught, it means that someone or something must be left out. Here lies the root of the problem: How do we prioritize what is and is not taught? If schools are a reflection of society, as many have argued, they should do a better job representing the diverse actors that make up society, and the curriculum should play a part in telling these various stories and traditions (Wills, 2019).

2.9 Mastery Learning

First proposed by Benjamin Bloom in 1968, mastery learning is an educational approach that suggests that students must achieve mastery of prerequisite knowledge and skills before learning more complex material. Unlike traditional methods, where the entire class is expected to learn simultaneously regardless of individual students' ability, mastery learning suggests that all students possess the aptitude to learn. Still, some may require more time to reach the objective. Nevertheless, the research supporting mastery learning is significant. For example, a meta-analysis of 108 controlled studies of upper elementary, high school, and college students found that mastery learning increases student academic performance, particularly for weaker students (Kulik, Kulik & Bangert-Drowns, 1990).

Teaching to mastery goes beyond simply "covering" material through the course of a lesson, hoping that students learned what they were supposed to. Instead, teaching to mastery focuses on what students learned and not what the teacher taught. There are several components of mastery teaching. The first is that teachers must communicate to their students clearly defined learning objectives. In other words, students must know precisely what they are required to know and be able to do as a result of the lesson or unit of study. Additionally, students must understand what mastery looks like and know when they reach it. An excellent way to communicate mastery to students is by providing them with examples of mastery-level achievement. This could be a completed project, a sample essay, or other artifacts of learning. Next, teachers should provide their students with multiple opportunities to reach mastery. Understanding that not all students will achieve mastery simultaneously, teachers allow students to take summative assessments as many times as needed to demonstrate that they have mastered the content. Lastly, teachers need to provide students with timely, ongoing feedback on their learning progress. Feedback should focus on the knowledge and skills teachers want students to master and is best accomplished using a rubric.

TEACHING STRATEGIES FOR MASTERY LEARNING

To master complex skills and concepts, students must first become proficient in the subskills that lead to mastery. For example, students need to master vocabulary, grammar, syntax, mechanics, voice, and style to write well. Additionally, students must be able to group and organize their thoughts logically and make sure their writing is well suited for the audience, purpose, and genre for which they are writing. Teachers' main difficulty in teaching to mastery is that many of these subskills have become automatic, and they take for granted that many students have not mastered them. Because teachers don't routinely think about subskills, they are challenging to communicate and teach to learners. However, several powerful strategies can help students master skills and content, such as scaffolding, student voice and choice, practice, and feedback.

SCAFFOLDING

Teachers should provide their students with scaffolding and support as they move from novice to mastery. The concept of scaffolding is based on the work of cognitive psychologist Lev Vygotsky and his theory of the zone of proximal development (ZPD). The ZPD refers to the area of learning between what a person can do on their own and what they can do with the assistance of a skilled partner. Based on the concept of ZPD, Jerome Bruner coined the term scaffolding in the 1970s and applied Vygotsky's theory to the educational setting. Scaffolding is when the teacher breaks up concepts and skills into manageable chunks and provides students enough support to guide them to mastery of complex concepts or tasks. In other words, scaffolding helps students bridge the gap between what they know and what they need to know. Scaffolding can be done with one-to-one teaching or in collaborative learning environments where students can observe, ask questions, and teach others content and skills.

TEACHING STRATEGY:

There are several ways that teachers can provide scaffolding to their students to help them reach mastery. One of the approaches I use, especially when introducing a new concept or skill, is to model the behavior I want students to have. For example, suppose I am teaching students how to effectively communicate with their peers in cooperative learning groups. In that case, I will role-play with another student how to get one's point across, what it looks like to listen actively, and how to engage in healthy dispute resolution. We cannot assume that all students possess effective communication skills, and they must be implicitly shown how to work well with their peers. Additionally, I model intellectual processes too by doing a think-aloud. A think-aloud is when the teacher verbally articulates their internal thinking as they engage in an area of learning. This approach is effective, especially when students learn a skill or concept consisting of several steps or components.

Another effective scaffolding technique is to ask students open-ended questions. Open-ended questions are questions that cannot be answered with a simple yes or no. They require students to reflect and produce in-depth answers. They are a perfect way for teachers to focus on a specific concept while allowing students to elaborate and communicate what they know. Teachers can use student responses to identify gaps in understanding and provide support to reach mastery targets. In addition to whole-class questioning strategies, teachers can put students into small discussion groups or use "shoulder buddies" to have students engage in small group discussions. This is an excellent way for students to think about and process new information and concepts.

Using students' prior knowledge about a topic is an excellent scaffolding strategy. Teachers should try to tap into what students already know by utilizing something familiar to explain new and unfamiliar ideas. For example, a foreign language teacher could tap into their students' understanding of English grammar to teach the concepts of verb tenses, articles, and noun genders. Analogies are an effective way to teach students new concepts. An analogy is simply a comparison between two things. For example, when I teach students about 9/11, I compare it to the attack on Pearl Harbor. While history does not repeat itself, it does rhyme, and it can help students understand how the nation responded to the surprise attack.

Visual aids are a helpful device to scaffold student learning to mastery. They are supplemental materials that give shape or form to words and thoughts and help learners understand concepts or processes. Some examples of common visual aids in the classroom include slideshows, models, pictures, videos, infographics, handouts, graphic organizers, concept maps, flashcards, and informational posters. Further, they have been shown to increase the learning process because students learn better when presented with multiple representations (Shabiralyani, Hasan, Hamad, & Iqbal, 2015). Visual aids are an excellent way for the teacher to get and retain students' attention and keep them focused, especially during a presentation or lecture. As a history teacher, I like to present my students with parchment reproductions of important primary sources such as the Declaration of Independence and the U.S. Constitution.

Scaffolding is essential when engaging students with big projects or activities that have multiple steps. This is because some students may become overwhelmed by the project's proportions. A strategy to help students tackle big projects is chunking. Chunking is simply breaking the project down into small manageable pieces. Approaching projects in this way makes the task a lot less intimidating. Students are more likely to stay engaged with the project when small portions are assigned at regular intervals rather than having the project due all at once with little to no support. Additionally, teachers can help students complete large projects by creating checkpoints throughout the project. Checkpoints or milestones are predetermined points along the project timeline to evaluate progress toward completion. Checkpoints, like chunking, keep students moving forward without overwhelming them.

2.10 Student Voice and Choice

In addition to scaffolding, teachers should provide students with "voice and choice" of high-quality, standards-based learning opportunities. According to the Center for American Progress, student voice is students' input regarding their educations and may include instructional topics, student learning styles, how schools are designed, and more. Student voice is critical to historically marginalized students such as Black, Latinx, American Indian, socioeconomically vulnerable students, and students with disabilities because these students have not traditionally had a seat at the table regarding their educations (Benner, Jeffrey, & Brown, 2019). However, research indicates that when students have agency, such as planning educational activities, their investment, ownership, and consequent learning significantly increase (Flutter 2006; Grace 1999; Wehmeyer & Sands 1998; Platz 1996). A meta-study conducted in 2008 of the effects of choice on student learning supports this conclusion and "results indicated that providing choice enhanced intrinsic motivation, effort, task performance, and perceived competence, among other outcomes" (Patall, Cooper, & Wynn, 2010).

TEACHING STRATEGY:

There are many ways that teachers can provide their student's voice and choice in the classroom. Of course, the degree of student autonomy that the teacher offers is dependent on the class and the individual learners and their levels of maturity, initiative, and responsibility. I like to provide my students with "choice projects" at the end of a unit of study in which they select the type of project they want to complete. I provide the students with detailed instructions and rubrics for each type of project. Students may choose to create a poster, display board, mural, diorama, poem, informational or documentary video, game, research paper, or they may choose to give an oral report. More autonomous students can submit a proposal for an original project as long as the project conforms to the unit's learning goals. I require that students creating an original project design a rubric to evaluate their work.

2.11 Practice

Practice makes perfect, but how much practice? In Malcolm Gladwell's 2008 best-seller, *Outliers: The Story of Success*, Gladwell points out that it takes approximately ten thousand hours of practice to achieve mastery of a given skill and quotes author and neurologist, Daniel Levitin to help explain, "The emerging picture from such studies is that ten thousand hours of practice is required to achieve the level of mastery associated with being a world-class expert—in anything." In study after study, of composers, basketball players, fiction writers, ice skaters, concert pianists, chess players, master criminals, and what have you, this number comes up again and again. Of course, this doesn't address why some people get more out of their practice sessions than others. But no one has yet found a case in which true world-class expertise was accomplished in less time. It seems that it takes the brain this long to assimilate all that it needs to know to achieve true mastery.

Research indicates that practice must be deliberate, meaning that it must be purposeful and systematic. Psychologist K. Anders Ericsson, a pioneer and leading researcher in expertise and human performance, suggests that all human beings can achieve mastery of a given domain through deliberate practice. Deliberate practice is different than regular practice in that through deliberate practice a practitioner breaks down a given task into its constituent parts or chunks. They then master the component parts through daily practice, usually accompanied by immediate coaching and feedback. Ericsson points out, "We argue that the differences between expert performers and normal adults reflect a life-long period of deliberate effort to improve performance in a specific domain" (Ericsson, Krampe, & Tesch-Römer, 1993). In other words, "Perfect practice results in perfect performance." Deliberate practice combined with grit and determination results in mastery far more often than innate talent alone. In addition to practice, teachers must provide students with consistent and timely feedback. Feedback is what teachers communicate to students about their academic progress toward learning goals and standards. Students, in turn, use the teacher's feedback to improve their learning.

2.12 Formative and Summative Assessment for Effective 21ˢᵗ Century Teaching

Assessments have different purposes in the 21st-century classroom. Some assessments are used to monitor and evaluate students learning during instruction. These are known as formative assessments. Assessments that measure what a student has learned at the end of a unit of instruction are summative assessments. Assessment is defined as the systematic collection, review, and use of information about educational programs undertaken to improve student learning and development (Marchese, 1987). Teachers must share all assessment data clearly and immediately with students to know their progress toward learning goals.

∎ FORMATIVE ASSESSMENTS FOR LEARNING

Formative assessments are assessments for learning. In other words, they provide a snapshot of where students are in their learning. According to James Popham, Emeritus professor in UCLA's Graduate School of Education, "Formative assessment is a process used by teachers and students during instruction that provides feedback to adjust ongoing teaching and learning to improve students' achievement on intended instructional outcomes" (2008, p. 5). Research indicates that formative assessment may be one of the most underrated but perhaps essential aspects of student achievement. For example, in an analysis of more than 250 studies, researchers Paul Black and Dylan Wiliam (1998) demonstrate the positive impact of assessment on student learning:

> The research reported here shows conclusively that formative assessment does improve learning. Moreover, the gains in achievement appear to be quite considerable, and as noted earlier, amongst the largest ever reported for educational interventions. As an illustration of just how big these gains are, an effect size of 0.7, if it could be achieved on a nationwide scale, would be equivalent to raising the mathematics attainment score of an "average" country like England, New Zealand or the United States into the "top five" after the Pacific rim counties of Singapore, Korea, Japan and Hong Kong (p. 61).

Robert Marzano (2010) points out that formative assessments can be either obtrusive or unobtrusive. Obtrusive assessments are when students are aware that they are being assessed. For example, in the middle of the lesson, the teacher stops instruction to administer a quiz to check for understanding. The teacher can use the quiz data to alter instruction as needed. On the other hand, unobtrusive assessments are assessments that are given discretely and sometimes without the students being aware they are being assessed. An example of an unobtrusive assessment is when the teacher elicits student responses during a class discussion for diagnostic purposes. The frequency of assessment is essential. Research indicates that for maximum student achievement, students should be assessed at least once a week, if not more (Marzano, 2006).

TEACHING STRATEGY:

A quick and easy way to gauge student learning is by asking students questions. It is important to sample as many students as possible to get a good feel of the class's understanding of a topic. To avoid having the same students answer all of the questions, I use the cold call method. Cold calling is when the teacher calls on a student who has not raised their hand. Research shows that when teachers utilize cold calling techniques, more students answer questions voluntarily, and the number of students answering questions increases over time. Further, in classes with high rates of cold calling, students become more comfortable participating in class discussions. Participation does not change in classrooms without cold calling (Dallimore, Hertenstein, & Platt, 2013). It is essential to be equitable when cold calling students. An excellent way to make sure that students are selected randomly is to use applications such as Wheel of Names, in which the teacher can load a class roster into a roulette-like spinning wheel that selects students at random. https://wheelofnames. com/

█ SUMMATIVE ASSESSMENTS OF LEARNING

Summative assessments are assessments of learning and measure student achievement in a given period. For example, summative assessments may be given at the end of a lesson, unit of study, quarter, semester, and school year. They are usually high stakes in that they significantly impact students' grades, and they are typically measured against state and district level standards and benchmarks. These types of tests are sometimes referred to as criterion-referenced tests because they assess a students' mastery of standards and benchmarks. According to Robert Stake, emeritus professor of education at the University of Illinois, a way to differentiate between formative and summative assessments is "When the cook tastes the soup, that's formative. When the guests taste the soup, that's summative." In traditional classrooms, summative assessments are usually administered as standardized tests such as multiple-choice, true and false, fill-in-the-blank, short- and long-form responses, or combinations thereof. Assessments of this type have several benefits. They are easy to grade, especially standardized test items administered electronically or graded with a scantron; they are objective and easy to create and administer; and they are a fast and convenient way to assess student achievement. There are criticisms of traditional standardized tests, however. One of the most common complaints is that standardized tests only evaluate students' low-level factual recall. These tests reinforce the notion that there can only be one "correct" answer and reduce complex and multifaceted subjects into one-dimensional solutions. As a result, these tests are not an accurate assessment of what students know and are able to do in real-life situations.

For assessments to be meaningful, they must be accurate reflections of the student's knowledge and competencies. To accurately interpret and communicate evaluations of student learning, the assessments must be both valid and reliable. Validity can be considered the "what" and "how" of assessment, while reliability addresses the "how well" of an assessment (Johnson, 2012). An assessment is considered valid when it accurately measures what it is supposed to measure. A test with a high degree of validity has test items closely tied to the test's focus. Reliability is the consistency of a test taker's performance on a given assessment. For example, if a student took multiple assessments on different days and achieved the same score, the assessment would be considered reliable. Many factors can influence the reliability and include selecting specific questions, grading the assessment, and even the day and time the student took the assessment.

▌ AUTHENTIC ASSESSMENTS

Authentic assessments, or performance-based assessments, are assessments that measure students' "intellectual accomplishments that are worthwhile, significant, and meaningful" (Newmann, Marks, & Gamoran, 1996). Authentic assessments are much more appropriate in the 21st-century classroom than traditional assessments because authentic assessments allow students to demonstrate their mastery of content and skills in an authentic, real-world setting. In other words, authentic assessments require students to exercise judgment, innovation, and creativity when applying what they have learned in a safe and supportive environment. In addition, authentic assessments require higher-level thinking skills and reflect what practitioners in the field do more accurately. This is opposed to the low-level factual recall common to traditional standardized tests (Wiggins & Mctighe, 2005). Finally, authentic assessments are excellent ways for students to engage in complex problem-solving and other 21st-century skills using various strategies such as role-playing, debates and simulations, project-based activities, extended research projects, experiments, case studies, and portfolios. According to Grant Wiggins (1998) an assignment is authentic if it

- is realistic
- requires judgment and innovation
- asks the student to "do" the subject
- replicates or simulates the contexts in which adults are "tested" in the workplace or in civic or personal life
- assesses the student's ability to efficiently and effectively use a repertoire of knowledge and skills to negotiate a complex task
- allows appropriate opportunities to rehearse, practice, consult resources, and get feedback on and refine performances and products.

Further, research has shown that authentic assessments increase student engagement, interest, critical thinking, and student achievement (Moria, Refnaldi, & Zaim, 2017; Sarya, Suarni, Adnyana, & Suastra, 2019). However, there are drawbacks to using authentic assessments, including pushback from students who may find them challenging due to the high cognitive demand and student collaboration. In addition, teachers may object to the increased time required to assess student learning and the lack of the resources needed to implement authentic assessments. However, with proper planning and foresight, many of these objections can be mitigated (Murphy, Fox, Freeman, & Hughes, 2017).

TEACHING STRATEGY:

When I teach my students about the U.S. Constitution, I point out that there are four amendments pertaining to voting. The fifteenth gives Black men the right to vote, the nineteenth provides for women's suffrage, the twenty-fourth eliminates the poll tax, and the twenty-sixth amendment allows eighteen-year-olds to vote. As an authentic assessment of student learning about the Constitution, the article five amendment process, and voter participation, I have my students research the pros and cons of lowering the voting age to sixteen. I then have them craft a bill and debate its merits in a congressional simulation. Students really get into the topic when they have an opportunity to do something "real" as opposed to traditional approaches. Authentic assessments are an excellent way to spark students' interest and develop 21st-century skills while engaged in meaningful hands-on learning.

2.13 Questions for Reflection

1. What are some examples of research-based teaching practices that have been shown to be effective at increasing student learning? How have you used these techniques in your own educational setting? Were they effective? Why or why not?

2. Describe the different kinds of knowledge that teachers must possess to be highly effective. What are some ways that teachers can increase their professional knowledge especially in those areas that they are weak in?

3. What is the difference between standards and curriculum? And how does the understanding of the different types of curricula help educators deliver equitable instruction?

4. Describe why mastery learning is important and the various components of mastery learning to include scaffolding, voice and choice, practice, and feedback.

5. What are the differences between formative and summative assessments? Describe when and how formative and summative assessments are best used.

Chapter

03

Effective Learning for the 21st Century

Tell me and I forget, teach me and I may remember, involve me and I learn.

—BENJAMIN FRANKLIN

There is no end to education. It is not that you read a book, pass an examination, and finish with education. The whole of life, from the moment you are born to the moment you die, is a process of learning.

—JIDDU KRISHNAMURTI

The illiterate of the 21st century will not be those who cannot read and write, but those who cannot learn, unlearn, and relearn.

—ALVIN TOFFLER

For apart from inquiry, apart from the praxis, individuals cannot be truly human. Knowledge emerges only through invention and re-invention, through the restless, impatient, continuing, hopeful inquiry human beings pursue in the world, with the world, and with each other.

-PAULO FREIRE, PEDAGOGY OF THE OPPRESSED

To create effective learners for the 21st-century, educators must take deliberate steps to develop within each student the ability to collaborate, solve unique and challenging problems, foster the spirit of inquiry, develop technological literacy, engage in multidisciplinary learning, and instill within each student educational agency and flexibility by creating learning activities that are meaningful and relevant. Teachers should offer students voice and choice based on their unique interests, knowledge, and skills. Students well-versed in these skills and dispositions will be able to meet and overcome the challenges of a future that will look radically different from the present. At the heart of an education for the 21st century is effective learning. According to the Merriam-Webster dictionary, learning is defined as "the knowledge or skill acquired by instruction or study." Students usually acquire knowledge and skills in schools due to their interactions with their teachers through well-designed learning activities. For effective learning to occur, teachers must possess the skills and attributions discussed in the last chapter. In addition, they must have a deep understanding of how students learn. Knowledge of teaching and learning is essential because they are not the same things. In other words, just because something was taught does not mean that students learned. According to Mary Immordino-Yang, associate professor of education, psychology, and neuroscience at University of Southern California, "We think of teachers conveying info and students receiving it, but that's not how humans learn [...] We need instead teachers who are trained to be thoughtful observers of the people around them and supporters of the adaptive behaviors that they see." In other words, teachers must understand how to teach effectively, but they must also know how students learn and apply that knowledge of human learning to maximize learning and student achievement.

Objectives:

- Describe the role memory plays in learning and how to increase students' retention of content.

- Describe active learning and why it is important for a 21st-century education.

- Describe the importance of developing students' entrepreneurial mindset for success in and out of the classroom.

⤴ Explain the benefits of educational technology to include blended learning.

⤴ Describe some of the persistent myths about how we learn.

⤴ Describe how educators can use action research to increase student learning through the six phases of inquiry.

3.1   Effective Learning

The precise definition of learning is challenging as many people have differing opinions about the causes, processes, and consequences of learning. The discrepancy may be because learning has been the subject of research in various disciplines, including psychology, cognitive science, neuroscience, education, and anthropology. Each examines the phenomenon through the lens of their fields of study. However, most education professionals agree that learning is an "enduring change in behavior, or in the capacity to behave in a given fashion, which results from practice or other forms of experience" (Schunk, 2012). Further, learning involves change, endures over time, and occurs through experience. Effective learning is a complex process that involves several interconnected elements, chief among them memory.

3.2   Memory

Most people associate learning with remembering academic content. Memory, therefore, plays a significant role in effective learning. The more we can get our students to remember what we teach, the better learners they are. There are two basic categories of memory: short-term and long-term. Short-term memory has a storage capacity of only about seven items and a duration of only a few dozen seconds. Techniques such as "chunking" information into small, easily learned groups, phrases, words, and numbers could help learners recall information in short-term memory more readily than unchunked information. For example, it may be challenging to memorize the sequence 78568956872, but it becomes easier to do if you chunk it to look like this 7856 895 6872. Long-term memories, on the other hand, have an almost unlimited capacity and duration. These are the memories we hold on to from our earliest childhoods or other occurrences in our distant pasts. In healthy functioning brains, the constraint on recalling our distant memories is not the availability of those memories but accessibility to them. Effective learning involves moving short-term memory into long-term memory through a process known as memory consolidation. In other words, memory consolidation is the process of making learning "stick." Memory consolidation involves structural and chemical changes in the nervous system, such as strengthening synaptic connections between neurons that connect various memories throughout the brain. These connections become more robust and faster over time, increasing the durability of long-term memory. Think of it as a path in the woods. The more often you walk down the trail, the easier it becomes to navigate. There are three critical strategies for moving short-term memories into long-term memory—they are repetition, imagery, and patterns, also known as RIP.

3.3   Repetition

According to Larry Squire, neurologist, and professor of psychiatry at the University of California in San Diego, repeated rehearsal at regular intervals is the best way to consolidate learning into long-term memory. As most teachers know, repetition is an essential strategy for long-term learning. However, too much repetition can get boring for students and teachers. To keep learning fresh and exciting, effective teachers use various techniques to make the repetition palatable. Some successful approaches include movement and dance, songs, raps, call and response, and games. These approaches are the sugar that helps make the medicine go down. They are great ways to learn effectively and have fun at the same time. In addition to teachers using these techniques with their classes, students should be taught how to use these techniques to help them become effective independent learners.

3.4 Imagery

Using imagery is an excellent mnemonic to improve memory. In a recent study at Georgia State University, participants were told to create mental images corresponding to conceptually related word lists. Those who made mental images representing the lists of words could recall more words than people who did not create images. For example, if a student is trying to remember the word *fulcrum*, they could imagine a glass "full of crumbs" resting on a teeter-totter. Researchers have found that the more exaggerated and sillier the mental images, the more likely we will remember them. When something is novel and different, it stands out from the routine and mundane. For example, you might have difficulty recalling what you had for dinner three weeks ago. Still, suppose that day was your birthday and you were surprised with a party. In that case, you might be more likely to remember other details, such as what was served for dinner (especially if it was your favorite dish).

Graphic organizers are another helpful way to use visual information. Graphic organizers are a pedagogical tool that visually depicts relationships between facts, concepts, and ideas. Some popular graphic organizers include concept mapping, sequence maps, Venn diagrams, and flowcharts. For instance, in a lesson on the American Revolution, students could create a sequence map illustrating the significant events leading to the Declaration of Independence, such as the Stamp Acts, the Boston Massacre, and the Boston Tea Party. To further strengthen their memory, students could include clip art or other representations for each cause.

▌VENN DIAGRAM

One of my favorite graphic organizers is the Venn diagram. The Venn diagram consists of two circles that overlap, forming three distinct areas. The two central regions help students identify characteristics that are unique to that specific topic or subject. In contrast, the area of overlap is used to determine things the two topics have in common. Thus, Venn diagrams are a valuable strategy to help students compare and contrast two disparate events or concepts while "seeing" their similarities.

T-CHART

T-charts are a simple but effective way for students to examine two distinct facets of a topic. Shaped like the capital letter T, students could use a T-chart to think about fact and opinion, advantages and disadvantages, or pros and cons of a topic.

CONCEPT MAP

A concept map is a visual representation of related ideas or concepts. It begins with a box or circle containing a central idea or notion. It then branches out, usually in a hierarchical downward direction showing how the main idea is related to its constituent parts, depicted by labeled arrows and circles.

SEQUENCE CHART

A sequence chart is a graphic organizer that lets students put events, steps, processes, or stories in sequential and visually appealing order. There are various ways for students to build sequence charts, but arrows pointing from one event to another is a practical approach.

TEACHING STRATEGY:

Graphic organizers are an excellent way to gather diagnostic information from students at the beginning of a lesson or to assess student learning during a lesson formatively. Students can quickly and easily create the graphic organizers above using paper and pencil or Google for Education tools such as Google Docs or Jamboard.

3.5 Patterns

The brain is optimized to seek and make sense out of the world by identifying patterns. Patterns are observations that individuals organize into meaningful categories. Patterns exist everywhere in our daily life, including mathematics, music, language, and nature. When we receive information about the world from our five senses, we search our brains for prior knowledge about the topic and a way to organize the information. If the information matches something we already know about, it strengthens already existing neural networks. This is called pattern recognition. Pattern recognition can significantly enhance learning because, as the old saying goes, "neurons that fire together, wire together."

TEACHING STRATEGY:

There are several ways to present information to students using patterns. One of my favorite ways to use patterns in the classroom is through music. Music contains both rhythmic and melodic patterns. Further, using music enhances relational teaching and is an excellent way to boost motivation, creativity, and joy. For example, when I teach about the Civil Rights Movement, I like to play Fannie Lou Hamer's "Go Tell It on the Mountain," Aretha Franklin's "Respect," and Sam Cooke's "A Change Is Gonna Come." Students are naturally pulled into the music, which helps them connect to the academic content emotionally. In addition to playing popular music, I have students create their own songs, raps, or spoken word to learn and review academic content. Students love to engage in creative work, and it is an excellent way to change things up and keep the lesson exciting and engaging.

3.6 Acronym

The acronym is another popular mnemonic that uses patterns. Acronyms use a letter to represent each word or phrase that needs to be remembered. For example, NFL stands for the National Football League. Acronyms can be used to remember all sorts of things, such as the MAIN causes of World War I: militarism, alliances, imperialism, and nationalism. Or to determine if an organism is living or nonliving, use the acronym MRS GREN to represent the seven life processes of movement, respiration, sensation, growth, reproduction, excretion, and nutrition. An acrostic is another valuable strategy to help students memorize content. In this approach, like the acronym, students associate letters with the concept to learn, but instead of creating a new word, students create a sentence. For example, music teachers can help their students remember the treble clef lines, EGBDF, using the acrostic Every Good Boy Does Fine. Likewise, students remember Please Excuse My Dear Aunt Sally to remember the order of operations in algebra: parentheses, exponents, multiplication, division, addition, and subtraction.

TEACHING STRATEGY:

Have students create acronyms or acrostics to memorize key concepts, facts, or processes. The wackier, the better, as students are more likely to remember things that stand out or are different and humorous. Teachers can utilize repetition, imagery, and patterns (RIP) to help students consolidate their learning into long-term memory by implementing the TRAP acronym. TRAP stands for translate, repeat, a picture, and practice.

T **Translate**
Have students translate the information or ideas into their own words. By making it their own, they are more inclined to remember the content.

R **Repeat**
Students should have the opportunity to repeat the information and relate the content to old concepts and new ones.

A **A picture**
They say that a picture is worth a thousand words. Have students visualize the information in their mind's eye.

P **Practice**
Students should have many opportunities to practice what they have learned. The more students practice, the more they will be able to recall.

3.7 Active Learning is the Key to a 21st Century Education

MIT linguistics professor Noam Chomsky once said that "It's not important what is covered in a class; it is what students discover." This approach to education should not be relegated to only students at elite institutions of higher learning. All students, K–16, should have the opportunity to tap into their natural-born curiosity through learning that ignites passion and a sense of wonder. In other words, students must possess agency in their learning and be actively engaged in the learning process. The Center for Educational Innovation defines active learning as "any approach to instruction in which all students are asked to engage in the learning process. Active learning stands in contrast to 'traditional' modes of instruction in which students are passive recipients of knowledge from an expert."

Active learning is not a new idea. Progressive education reformer John Dewey called for changes to the public education system over one hundred years ago. The 19th-century philosopher, psychologist, and education reformer believed that education should be an experiential process. Students should have the opportunity to take an active role in their learning. According to Dewey, the purpose of education is not just to teach students vast amounts of predetermined knowledge but for students to realize their full potential by using their knowledge and skills for the common good through the participation in democratic classrooms. As Dewey once said, "Give the pupils something to do, not something to learn; and the doing is of such a nature as to demand thinking; learning results naturally." In addition to Dewey, Jean Piaget, Jerome Bruner, Ernst von Glaserfeld, and Lev Vygotsky expanded the idea of student-centered instruction when they developed constructivist learning theory.

Constructivism is a learner-centered approach that suggests that students actively "construct" their knowledge. Each individual's reality is determined by their prior knowledge, beliefs, and experiences. Because learning is based on personal experiences, each student's learning is unique to them. In other words, "Constructivist approaches emphasize learners actively constructing their own knowledge rather than passively receiving information transmitted to them from teachers and textbooks. From a constructivist perspective, knowledge cannot simply be given to students: Students must construct their own meanings" (Stage, Muller, Kinzie and Simmons, 1998, p. 35). Constructivist learning theory is based on numerous principles, such as students learn by doing. When students have agency in their learning, they build their capacity as learners and improve in their abilities, skills, and expertise. Additionally, constructivists believe that learning is a social activity best accomplished when students are engaged in activities involving their peers, families, and communities to solve problems and accomplish learning tasks. Learning is contextual, and teachers must design learning activities that consider students' prior knowledge, beliefs, and experiences. Finally, constructivists believe that students' intrinsic motivation is the key to effective learning and student engagement. Students will not learn appropriately if they are not motivated to do so. Hands-on, active learning, and student-centered methods have given rise to a wide variety of pedagogical techniques that foster active learning, personalization, and collaboration.

Linda Darling-Hammond, the Charles E. Ducommun Professor of Education Emeritus at the Stanford Graduate School of Education and the president and CEO of the Learning Policy Institute, is a leading expert in education policy and practice. In her more than five hundred articles and twenty-five published books, Darling-Hammond repeatedly points out that meaningful learning is achieved when students actively participate in their educations. She points out that inquiry learning styles, such as project-based, design-based, and problem-based approaches, are highly effective ways to engage students. A growing body of research in student-centered approaches indicates that when students have the opportunity to apply their learning to real-world situations using collaborative methods, they learn more deeply. Additionally, active learning can more profoundly impact student performance than any other variable, including the student's background and prior achievement. And students are overall more successful when shown how to learn, not just what to learn (Darling-Hammond et al., 2015). Unfortunately, many students, especially in the upper grades, are seldom allowed to participate in their learning actively. As a result, education is done to them, rather than something that they do for themselves.

Passive learning has led to an "engagement cliff" where students fall off the mountain of interest as they transition from elementary to middle and high school. To illustrate the problem, a 2016 Gallop Poll of more than three thousand schools across the country documented the steep decline of upper school engagement when it reported that 74 percent of surveyed fifth graders said they were engaged in school. However, only 32 percent of eleventh graders reported being involved. According to the Harvard Graduate School of Education, there are many reasons why students grow bored of school. But perhaps the most significant reason when they transition from the lower grades to the upper grades is that students in the lower grades spend a lot of time participating in tactile and creative learning. In comparison, students in the higher grades receive instruction that is cerebral and regimented. In other words, education goes from being "child-centered to subject-centered."

According to the National Center for Education Statistics, all races' national high-school dropout rate had decreased from 9.7 percent in 2006 to 5.3 percent in 2018. And while this is cause for celebration, there should still be about 1.2 million students who left school early without earning a degree. That's approximately one student every twenty-six seconds or 7,000 dropouts every day. A study conducted by Indiana University of more than eighty-one thousand students in 110 high schools across twenty-six states, mainly in the Midwest, examined the dropout problem. And while not a national survey, the data is consistent with national trends in American education. In trying to determine why high school students disengage from school and entertain thoughts of dropping out, 73 percent of students responded, "I didn't like the school." Sixty-one percent said, "I didn't like the teachers." Sixty percent said, "I didn't see the value in the work I was being asked to do." When asked what students want to see change at school, overwhelmingly, students responded that they want more interactive classes with the interaction between teachers and peers. In other words, students want to be actively engaged in their learning—creating, drawing, diagnosing, assessing, and solving problems—not passive bystanders.

3.8 Inquiry-Based Learning

Inquiry-based learning (IBL), broadly defined, is an educational approach that puts students at the center of their learning. Instead of being passive recipients of the teacher's knowledge, students take an active role in their educations by asking questions, conducting research, and creating arguments based on evidence. This approach challenges traditional norms of the teacher-centered classroom in which the teacher is the source of all knowledge or the "sage on the stage." Instead, in an inquiry-based classroom, the teacher is the "guide on the side." In other words, the teacher facilitates and advises the students as they "discover" the answers to questions and construct their knowledge and understanding of the world. Through active inquiry and discovery, students become motivated to learn because they seek answers to questions that interest them rather than facts that have to be memorized. In addition, inquiry learning usually occurs in small cooperative learning groups, so students gain valuable experience working as team members. Collaboration is an essential 21st-century skill that builds students' communication and decision-making skills and their ability to contribute ideas and energy to support the group.

There are many forms of IBL, but in an analysis of the inquiry process such as those found at the Harvard Social Studies Project and the Amherst Project, researchers have identified three main components of inquiry instruction; namely, questions, tasks, and sources (Swan, Grant, & Lee, 2019). Good questions drive the inquiry process. The discipline-based questions can come from either students or the teacher. According to Jay McTighe and Grant Wiggins in their book *Essential Questions* (2013), they are essential because "the use of questions signals to students that inquiry is the goal of learning in your class, and makes it more likely that a unit of study will be intellectually engaging." Additionally, "the use of questions forces us to clarify and prioritize what is truly important in terms of learning outcomes for our students." In other words, for teachers to be successful in this approach, they must be reflective and thoughtful practitioners and reduce into its simplest form the main learning objectives in terms of knowledge and skills. For students engaging in the inquiry process, questions help ignite their curiosity and generate interest in the task. Questions drive the project, and it helps the student answer the question: "Why are we doing this?"

Tasks in the inquiry-based classroom are used to monitor and assess student learning. Formative tasks provide teachers with information about student learning and understanding during the inquiry process. They can help teachers keep students on the right path of inquiry in terms of knowledge and skills. If students begin to veer off-topic, the teacher can quickly respond and help the students regain focus. In inquiry learning, formative tasks are usually in the form of supporting questions. Some other formative tasks include student-led discussions in either small learning groups or the whole class setting. Student portfolios, learning journals, and self-reflections are other practical formative tasks that can give teachers immediate feedback on student progress. Conversely, summative tasks require students to demonstrate their learning by responding to the driving question posed at the beginning of the unit of study. Ideally, the summative assessment will be an authentic application of the knowledge and skills learned in the lesson that will allow students to exercise judgment and innovation while completing a real-world task.

The last component of inquiry learning is sources. Source evidence for inquiry learning should consist of primary sources. Primary sources were created during the period under investigation or created afterward by someone who witnessed the event. Primary sources include newspaper articles, governmental documents, official and unofficial correspondence, maps, speeches, memoirs, music, art, photographs, movies, documentaries, audio recordings, and interviews. Using various sources from multiple viewpoints is crucial because it helps students understand the complexity of their topic by engaging them in historical thinking and authentic learning. Interpreting primary sources requires students to think about the importance of authorship, intended audience, bias, and purpose of the source. Further, primary sources let students reach their conclusions about a historical event rather than be told about it in a textbook. However, secondary and tertiary sources such as encyclopedias, books, and articles can be appropriate, especially at the beginning stages of research when students try to understand the topic.

Inquiry learning is flexible enough to meet the needs of almost every teacher and learning scenario. The approach can be used in all subjects as the primary instruction or add-on to the traditional curriculum. There are four types of inquiry that teachers can implement depending on their students' academic needs, experience, motivation, and ability to work independently or as collaborative teams. The four types of inquiry are limited inquiry, structured inquiry, guided inquiry, and open inquiry (Banchi & Bell, 2008). Limited inquiry is the least complex because it requires teachers to construct and lead their students through the inquiry with a predetermined procedure and outcome. The next type of inquiry is structured inquiry. It is similar to the confirmation inquiry, except that the final product is unknown. In a structured inquiry, the teacher prepares in advance all driving questions, sources, and explicit step-by-step instructions at each stage of the inquiry. Students will then think critically to arrive at an answer to the driving question. The last type of inquiry is open inquiry. In this type of inquiry, students develop the driving question, formative and summative performance tasks, and locate all source evidence for the investigation. The teacher's role is to support their students along the way by acting as a guide or mentor. Open inquiry is the highest expression of student learning because the student is responsible for most of the heavy intellectual lifting. They ask their questions and find answers to their questions independently.

With the continued emphasis in American schools on standardized test scores, data-driven instruction, and other quantifiable measures of student learning, many educators may be reluctant to incorporate IBL in their classrooms. The fear is that time taken away from the traditional curriculum based on rote memorization and drill, and practice approaches will lower test performance. Research indicates, however, that incorporating inquiry learning increases student test scores and does not lower them. For example, a study of seventh- and eighth-grade students in the Detroit Public School system examined the impact of a project-based inquiry science unit on student achievement. The study revealed significant gains in science content and the scientific process measured by state standardized science tests. The increases in learning have been attributed to greater student interest and participation in the topic, especially for traditionally underserved urban students (Geirt et al., 2008). Another study analyzed IBL's impact on students' critical thinking skills in science and technology. Students engaged in an IBL-based lesson increased their critical thinking skills and overall positive attitude toward science and technology (Duran & Dökme, 2016). Further, students who engaged in IBL have been shown to experience upward of 40 percent growth according to pretest/posttest analysis (Witt & Ulmer, 2010).

These findings are not an aberration but represent the literature that consistently supports the positive impacts of IBL and constructivist approaches on student learning.

One of the perennial challenges in education policy is implementing change. As the American inventor, engineer, and businessman Charles Kettering once said, "The world hates change, yet it is the only thing that has brought progress." As uncomfortable as change can be, it is necessary so that every student has access to a 21st-century education. Student-centered approaches like IBL have been shown to increase student achievement and develop 21st-century skills through active learning and engagement. These skills and dispositions are vitally needed if our students are going to succeed in the knowledge economy. Yet despite the evidence to the contrary, many stakeholders balk at the necessity of adopting contemporary pedagogical approaches. There are many reasons why change is difficult to implement, but fear of the unknown may be the leading culprit. People fear what they don't understand and that includes new approaches to teaching and learning. Change that threatens the status quo may be perceived as a threat to teachers' power, autonomy, and, in many cases, their emotional well-being. Change can cause severe anxiety. Just ask any teacher who had to convert to 100 percent online teaching during the COVID-19 quarantine. Teaching for a 21st-century education is transformational for both students and teachers. In other words, when teachers engage their students in 21st-century learning like IBL, they are providing them with the knowledge, skills, and dispositions to become critical thinkers and lifelong learners. IBL benefits the teacher too because they have more opportunities to collaborate with their students. Since class time is not filled with lectures and worksheets, teachers will have time to develop relationships with their students. However, as beneficial as IBL is, it is not without criticism.

3.9 Challenges Implementing IBL

One of the main concerns teachers have with inquiry learning is time. Teachers are naturally concerned with allocating time to learning activities that don't "cover" as many standards as traditional approaches. In the current educational milieu of standards-based teaching and high-stakes tests, this is a significant concern for many teachers because they don't want their students to "fall behind" or worry that they will not be prepared. Another problem is that inquiry learning can be noisy and chaotic, primarily when students work in collaborative teams. In the traditional classroom, the teacher is the source of all knowledge, and students are simply vessels that need to be filled up. This process is orderly, and classrooms are quiet except for teacher talk. In student-centered classrooms, on the other hand, students engage with one another in groups, which creates noise levels that could be interpreted as unruly and a loss of teacher control and discipline. As mentioned before, in the inquiry classroom, the teacher's role is to be a "guide on the side" instead of the "sage on the stage." This fundamental change in the teachers' role could be difficult for some teachers as many are unwilling to give up power and control. However, this paradigm shift is an integral component of student-centered instruction.

Evaluating IBL is another challenge. This is partly because the educational philosophy behind IBL suggests that there may be a spectrum of correct answers depending on the complexity of the inquiry. Unlike traditional assessments, such as multiple-choice, true and false, and matching items that distill complex ideas into a single correct answer, IBL should be evaluated using authentic assessments. Authentic assessments allow students to demonstrate their learning by engaging in activities requiring acquired knowledge and skills to real-world situations and problems. Discovering creative solutions to the driving question is what gives IBL is educative value. However, due to the subjective nature of the assessment, teachers must use standards-based rubrics throughout the lesson and communicate all expectations to students. Ideally, this is done before the students begin the inquiry. Other challenges of assessing IBL include grading individual performance and group outcomes and the time it takes to grade student work effectively.

IBL is about what students learned at the end of the lesson and how they learned it. In other words, students, not the teacher, shoulder the responsibility for their learning. This is in stark contrast to traditional passive learning, where the teacher does most of the work. Another way of thinking about it is that students, not the teacher, should leave school every day feeling mentally exhausted. Because the traditional "sit and get" approach is easier for the student, many will push back against doing the intellectual heavy lifting required of IBL. Additionally, it will be incumbent on teachers to communicate the unique expectations of IBL to all stakeholders, including students, families, and administration. IBL is not a traditional educational approach and may be met with skepticism by those who don't understand its principles. Teachers should be ready to briefly and directly explain why they are implementing IBL and how it will benefit students.

TEACHING STRATEGY:

My interests in inquiry learning and culturally responsive teaching (see chapter 5) resulted in synthesizing the two approaches I call culturally responsive inquiry learning or CRIL. CRIL is a student-centered pedagogical approach based on the inquiry model of learning. CRIL places high cognitive demand on learners as they ask their own questions, seek answers to those questions, present their findings, and develop critical consciousness by engaging in informed action. To see an example of a CRIL lesson, visit: https://docs. google.com/document/d/1O-UB8IAtYrhbSFHPvh4f2_mOb192hp3F/ edit?usp=sharing&ouid=109167993240480766180&rtpof=true&sd=true

3.10 Entrepreneurial Mindset

In her landmark book *Mindset: The New Psychology of Success*, world-renowned Stanford psychologist Carol Dweck outlines the importance of mindset as an integral component of success. Dweck defines *mindset* as a "self-perception or "self-theory" that people hold about themselves. Dweck contends that success is achieved with more than raw talent and abilities. Human beings can grow and strengthen their innate capabilities through the application of a "growth mindset." Dweck points out, "In a growth mindset, people believe that their most basic abilities can be developed through dedication and hard work—brains and talent are just the starting point. This view creates a love of learning and a resilience that is essential for great accomplishment" (Dweck, 2015). Mindset is essential to success because calibrated correctly, it can lead to opportunities, inspire creativity, fire up the desire to do something great, and improve quality of life. But the opposite is also true, "In a fixed mindset, people believe their basic qualities, like their intelligence or talent, are simply fixed traits. They spend their time documenting their intelligence or talent instead of developing them. They also believe that talent alone creates success—without effort" (Dweck, 2015). Mindset is a critical factor in the success of entrepreneurs. As T.V. personality, actress, producer, author, and businesswoman Oprah Winfrey points out, "Every time you state what you want or believe, you're the first to hear it. It's a message to both you and others about what you think is possible. Don't put a ceiling on yourself." One of Winfrey's keys to success is her ability to think entrepreneurially and utilize a growth mindset. An entrepreneurial mindset is not just for business leaders, however. Educators can learn essential lessons from entrepreneurs, such as developing their students' entrepreneurial mindset so that they can go boldly into the world, effect change, create value, and borrow from Apple Inc's 1997 advertising slogan, "Think different."

The word entrepreneur comes from the French word *entreprendre*, which means to "undertake." An entrepreneur is defined as someone who organizes and operates a business based on an idea or product they created, usually at great personal financial peril. In other words, entrepreneurs reap great monetary rewards when they are successful but risk financial failure when they are not. Entrepreneurs can positively impact society by creating businesses, goods, and services that contribute to economic growth, poverty alleviation, revenue generation, and wealth and job creation. Further, entrepreneurs can transform innovative ideas into valuable goods and services in both the for-profit and nonprofit sectors to make the world a better place (Kouakou, Li, Akolgo, & Tchamekwen, 2019). The United States has produced some of the world's most successful and impactful entrepreneurs. Individuals such as Andrew Carnegie, Thomas Edison, Henry Ford, and Steve Jobs helped propel the nation to economic preeminence by thinking outside of the box and taking risks to create revolutionary products and services. History remembers these exceptional businessmen as mavericks, individuals who changed the world through hard work, perseverance, and a little bit of luck. What this narrative misses, however, is that while most entrepreneurs possess certain innate traits, they must learn many more along the way to be successful. As *Forbes* magazine points out, there is no such thing as a "one-man band" in entrepreneurship. In other words, entrepreneurs need to learn new skills and dispositions that will help them be successful throughout their careers, usually through experience, study, and reflection, and often with the guiding hand of a mentor. The good news is that most people can learn to cultivate their entrepreneurial mindset to achieve their personal and professional goals. The most successful entrepreneurs are the ones who are on a personal journey of self-actualization and improvement. As the best-selling author and speaker Derric Yuh Ndim points out, "Personal growth is the most powerful force for change on earth. I believe that personal growth can help anyone change anything."

An entrepreneurial mindset is when the two concepts of entrepreneurship and mindset merge into one. It is how someone thinks about and sees the world and how these perceptions shape their entrepreneurial attitudes. In other words, it is how someone analyzes the world and the opportunities and the possibilities in it (Reed & Stoltz, 2011). According to the Network for Teaching Entrepreneurship (NFTE), eight domains comprise an entrepreneurial mindset—they are:

Future Orientation	Students acquire the knowledge, skills, and dispositions that will help them transition to college, career, and civic life.
Comfort With Risk	Students gain confidence working in an uncertain and challenging environment. They can make good decisions under pressure and uncertainty.
Opportunity Recognition	Students see problems as opportunities to create solutions, not setbacks.
Initiative and Self-Reliance	Students develop as independent learners who take ownership of their successes and failures. They require a minimum of input and guidance to solve their own problems.
Communication and Collaboration	Students can effectively communicate to diverse audiences verbally and in writing. They can persuade others to work collaboratively toward a common goal.
Creativity and Innovation	Students can analyze problems from various perspectives with empathy and propose novel solutions.
Critical Thinking and Problem-Solving	Students can develop creative solutions to problems, usually under uncertain circumstances.
Flexibility and Adaptability	Students work well in a rapidly changing world by changing plans and adapting to new challenges.

An entrepreneurial mindset is not just beneficial to business leaders and those wishing to build a start-up. There is great power in teaching young people to think entrepreneurially. This is because when students adopt an entrepreneurial mindset, they can live a better, more productive, and fulfilling life by embracing the attitudes and dispositions that can lead to success, such as grit, self-efficacy, and intrinsic motivation to succeed. For example, according to a longitudinal study conducted by the National Research Council, students with entrepreneurial skills such as creative problem-solving and effective collaboration were more likely to experience academic growth than students who did not possess those skills (Pellegrino & Hilton, 2013). Further, the Washington D.C. Children and Youth Investment Corporation reported that students who received entrepreneurial mindset instruction "improved academic performance, school attendance, and educational attainment" (Bronte-Tinkew & Redd, 2001).

Luckily for all of us, an entrepreneurial mindset is something that can be taught and learned. Although noncognitive skills such as critical thinking, problem-solving, perseverance, and teamwork are malleable, they are not "set in stone at birth and determined solely by genes. They can be fostered. Cognitive and noncognitive skills change with age and with instruction" (Kautz, 2014). Teachers can help students cultivate an entrepreneurial mindset by providing students with entrepreneurial learning experiences that allow students to engage in authentic, experiential, hands-on learning activities that require students to work cooperatively, such as inquiry learning, project-based learning, simulations, and role-playing techniques. An important concept for students to learn in developing an entrepreneurial mindset is that it is OK to fail. Traditionally, students are taught that success is defined by having all of the correct answers, but having an entrepreneurial mindset means that failing is perfectly acceptable. In fact, it is desirable. Henry Ford once quipped, "The only real mistake is the one from which we learn nothing." In other words, failure is an integral part of success. But it is what you do with that failure that makes a difference. Students need to learn to fail forward. In his viral Instagram video, titled "Fail early, fail often, fail forward," Will Smith encourages viewers that "You've gotta take a shot, you have to live at the edge of your capabilities. You gotta live where you're almost certain you're going to fail. Failure actually helps you to recognize the areas where you need to evolve. So fail early, fail often, fail forward."

3.11 Educational Technology for Effective Learning

According to the U.S. Department of Education, educational technology, or edtech, is "Used to support both teaching and learning, technology infuses classrooms with digital learning tools, such as computers and handheld devices; expands course offerings, experiences, and learning materials; supports learning 24 hours a day, 7 days a week; builds 21st-century skills; increases student engagement and motivation; and accelerates learning." When teachers effectively utilize computer technology in the learning environment, they can positively impact student achievement. For example, a meta-analysis of fifteen years of research conducted by Binbin Zheng, an assistant professor of educational psychology and special education at Michigan State University, revealed that one-to-one laptop usage had a statistically significant positive impact on students' English/language arts, writing, math, and science (Herold, 2016). Further, an analysis of eighty-six additional papers concerning educational technology pointed out other positive aspects of its use in the classroom, including increased technology use, more student-centered learning such as project-based learning, greater student engagement, and better relationships between students and their teachers. All of these things are essential to delivering an effective education for the 21st century.

Edtech can be a powerful way to increase student learning and achievement because teachers can use it in several practical ways. First, edtech can instruct and tutor students when the platform is used to help students understand new and complex concepts. A popular example is the Khan Academy. Developed by Salman Khan in 2006, the Khan Academy is a free online education platform that houses over 6,500 instructional videos ranging in a variety of academic subjects. Students can use the instructional videos asynchronously to either supplement or supplant in-school learning. In other words, student learning is not limited to time and space in a school. Instead, students are free to learn whenever and wherever is most convenient for them. Edtech can be an effective teaching tool when teachers use it to instruct students and incorporate various hardware and software platforms. Edtech hardware includes computers and printers, including 3D printers, tablets and laptops, interactive whiteboards, computer and document projectors, and virtual reality goggles. Software applications may consist of learning management systems (LMS) and a whole host of online tools that teachers can use to deliver instruction, such as cloud-based presentation applications, learning games, and instructional video. Lastly, edtech is an education tool when students use it to create content. Some examples of student-created content are websites, blogs, vlogs, podcasts, narrated slideshows, and digital storytelling, to name a few. When students create content for the web, they take ownership of their learning. They become part of a community of learners that can reach a worldwide audience.

For edtech to be effective, students must have the opportunity to go beyond technology that enhances learning to applications that transform learning, according to Dr. Ruben R. Puentedura. Dr. Puentedura is the founder and current president of Hippasus, an education technology consulting firm and developer of the SAMR model. SAMR stands for substitution, augmentation, modification, and redefinition. At the most basic level of SAMR, edtech is used as a substitution for traditional approaches without changing the function. For example, students use a laptop computer to take notes instead of using traditional pen and paper. The next higher level, augmentation, occurs when teachers use the technology as a direct substitution for conventional tasks but with some functional change. An example of this is when students take notes using a laptop computer but then use editing functions, clip art, hyperlinks, and embedded video to augment their notes, making them more dynamic and interactive. Finally, modification is when teachers use technology to redesign learning tasks. This is the level when edtech moves from the enhancement of learning to the transformation of learning. In other words, modification is an approach to edtech that allows students to solve old problems with new solutions. For example, instead of writing an informational essay, students could create an animated whiteboard-style explainer video or podcast complete with introductory music and sound effects. Redefinition is the highest level of edtech classroom integration and involves approaches that would have been impossible without technology. An example of redefinition is when students create a blog and post their research, commentary, and even student-made documentary videos. Students could take this a step further and solicit feedback from other students across their district, state, country, and even the world.

The SAMR framework is a valuable tool to help teachers think about their application of edtech. However, there are some criticisms of the model. First, it has been noted that there is a lack of empirical support in the peer-reviewed literature that SAMR produces student academic achievement. Further, SAMR focuses on the outcome and not the educative process involved in creating the product (Hamilton, Rosenberg, & Akcaoglu, 2016). While student achievement data may be lacking, it is anecdotally evident that when students use edtech to its highest potential, they become engaged in their learning while learning the skills and dispositions necessary for effective 21st-century learning.

What I've learned: Teaching through the COVID-19 pandemic and quarantine was not easy. Like many educators, I found myself teaching in a virtual environment almost overnight with little preparation and training to transition from in-person to virtual teaching. One of the biggest obstacles for me was learning the hardware and software to teach remotely. Before the quarantine, I had little understanding or experience with Google Meets or Zoom. I am not that familiar with the hardware side of computing, and I only had a basic grasp of computer video and sound. In addition, I had never designed a course using a learning management system (LMS), and I only had a rudimentary understanding of online learning tools. I am not a Luddite, but going from casual computer user to online teacher was a giant leap for me. There were many sleepless, stressed-filled nights during those first several weeks of distance learning as I tried to design and teach online for the first time. I was truly in crisis mode.

Besides the technical side, the most challenging part of distance learning was not being in the classroom with my students. Despite trying to engage them with icebreaker activities and various other attempts at getting to know them, I found it extremely difficult to connect with them personally the way I had in the physical classroom. In my opinion, there is no substitute for face-to-face contact when trying to build relationships. In addition, the teaching process is hampered when teaching remotely. I liken the experience to flying a plane by its instruments rather than by sight. Meaning that teachers depend on student nonverbals when teaching a lesson. Reading students' body language to see if they understand a concept is a fundamental teaching skill that is hampered when teachers cannot see their students because they are unable or refuse to turn on their cameras. In this scenario, teachers only have the data provided through various formative and summative assessments to guide their instruction. Further, situational awareness, or understanding what is going on in the classroom at all times, is almost impossible to do well in a remote teaching setting. Finally, teachers cannot use their physical proximity and voice dynamics to keep students focused and on task.

Despite the challenges of remote teaching, several positive outcomes came from the experience. As a result of the COVID-19 quarantine, school districts made a mad scramble to provide one-to-one computers to their students. A recent EdWeek Research Center survey found that 90 percent of educators polled indicated that their school had issued a laptop to every high schooler and middle school student by March of 2021. Elementary teachers reported that 84 percent of their students had a school computer. In addition to the challenges of ensuring every student had the appropriate technology and connectivity, many teachers received a crash course in distance learning, including how to use a learning management system, or LMS, to deliver online content to students. LMSs allow teachers to create, organize, administer, document, and track student learning using various online tools and analytics. Some of the most popular LMSs include Canvas, Schoology, and Google Classroom. In addition to using LMSs, many teachers became proficient at using various digital tools such as the Google Workspace for Education suite, including Google Docs, Forms, and Drive.

Now that most students have returned to in-person school, the question is whether teachers will continue to deploy online tools in what is known as blended learning. Sometimes referred to as hybrid or mixed learning, blended learning is when the teacher combines synchronous in-person teaching with asynchronous online tools to deliver content and instruction. Research has shown that students benefit when teachers employ blended learning. The approach has been shown to increase student engagement and learning by facilitating independent and collaborative learning opportunities and developing students' digital literacy skills (Rafiola, Setyosari, Radjah, & Ramli, 2020). Further, research indicates that students have an overall favorable view of blended learning (Alsalhi, Eltahir, & Al-Qatawneh, 2019) because it allows them to use apps, games, programs, and various digital media to learn at their own pace, allowing students to engage with content on their schedules, independent of when they are physically in the classroom. This, in turn, reduces students' stress, increases their satisfaction, and leads to deeper learning.

Besides increases in student engagement and achievement, blended learning saves money and resources by reducing the amount of paper used in the classroom. According to a recent survey, the typical American teacher uses between 25 and 75 pieces of paper every day for tests, homework, and other resources. A school typically uses about 360,00 pieces of paper per school year at an annual cost of $16,000. Nationally that translates to 32 billion pieces of paper used every year at the expense of $1.6 billion. Almost all of my assignments, handouts, and resources are now provided to students via LMS or Google Docs, cutting my copy paper consumption by approximately 90 percent. Not only does going digital save money, but it also saves time. I no longer have to prepare resources for printing or waste precious class time passing them out to students. Additionally, because students submit their assignments through the LMS, I don't have to carry piles of paper home to grade, and I have the convenience of grading students' work anytime and anyplace I want. Additionally, using an LMS makes learning accessible to students who are unable to come to school. Assuming the student has the appropriate technology and access to the Internet. Students will never fall behind in a blended learning environment because they cannot attend school in person. Further, building a course in an LMS requires the teacher to be organized and thoughtful. Teachers must be reflective practitioners when thinking about sequencing concepts, assignments, and activities and how students access and utilize them. I found transitioning my courses to online learning an excellent opportunity to reflect and critically analyze my curriculum. Instead of doing what I have always done, I had the chance to reevaluate my approach and optimize students learning by taking advantage of digital tools and resources. Another benefit to blended learning is that the courses are transparent. This means that families can see what their students are learning, including the assignments, activities, resources, and due dates. This is an excellent way to build bridges between the school and students' families, keep them engaged in their student's learning, and provide direct communication through the LMS.

Finally, K–12 students will benefit from blended learning because distance and blended learning have become the norm on most college campuses. A survey of 232 college faculty members across the country revealed that 73 percent utilize blended learning, while 12 percent teach entirely online. Further, the National Center for Education statistics reported that in the fall of 2019, there were 7,313,623 students enrolled in distance education courses at degree-granting colleges and universities. That translates to approximately 37 percent of all college students taking at least one online class. K–12 teachers who utilize blended learning approaches in their courses are preparing their students for the future as the number of courses and programs colleges offer online is only increasing. For example, since 2020, 98 percent of universities have reported that they provide online classes, and 75 percent of schools polled are investing in online technology to expand and improve their online course offerings. Currently, over 2,500 colleges offer fully online degree programs, with over three million students graduating from college never having stepped foot on campus. From associate degrees to doctoral level programs, online learning is growing in popularity. The online education market is forecasted to swell to over $350 billion by 2025.

Rahm Emanuel, former chief of staff under President Barrack Obama, famously said during the 2008 financial crisis, "You never want a serious crisis to go to waste." While stated in much different circumstances, this advice could be applied to schools and blended learning. This means that the transition to blended and fully online programs, due to the COVID quarantine, is an excellent opportunity for the field of education to evolve to a more high-tech future. However, although we have the chance to reimagine the possibilities and build on what we have collectively learned, we should not waste it by drifting back to the status quo.

3.12 Myths about how we Learn

Much of what teachers know about learning is the result of tradition, personal judgment, and experience, not evidenced-based best practices. A recent study indicates that "teachers' beliefs are often guided by subjective experience rather than by empirical data" (Fleckenstein, Johanna & Zimmermann, Friederike & Köller, Olaf & Möller, Jens 2015). In other words, teachers do what they have always done, regardless of whether the approach has educative value or is substantiated by educational research. The story of the pot roast best exemplifies the mindset and problem of teaching in this manner. As the story goes, a young woman hosts a dinner party for a few of her friends. The main dish being served that night was a delicious pot roast. Upon serving the roast and taking a bite, one of the woman's friends exclaimed how delicious it was and immediately asked her for the recipe. The host, flattered by the request, wrote down the recipe for her friend. Looking over their notes, her friend asked quizzically, "Why do you cut off both ends of the roast before putting it into the pan?" The woman replied, "I am not sure; I learned this recipe from my mother, and she always did it that way." The next day, the woman began thinking about her friend's question, and she decided to call her mother to find out. "Mom, why do you cut off the ends of the roast before placing it in the pan to cook?" Her mother responded, "I am not sure; I learned this recipe from your grandmother many years ago, and this is the way that she always did it." Now the woman was really curious. The next day she decided to call her elderly grandmother. "Grandma, Mom told me that you taught her to cut off the ends of the pot roast before cooking it. I have to know, why do you do that?" she asked quizzically. "Does cutting off the ends make the roast more tender and flavorful?" The grandmother paused for a long moment as she tried to remember the recipe, as she had not used it in quite some time. She finally responded. "I cut off both ends of the roast because the pan I had at the time was too small to fit the entire thing." This story exemplifies a fallacy in which most teachers engage. Because a lesson, technique, or approach has always been used, it must be empirically sound. Instead of critically evaluating their methodologies, most teachers simply do what they have always done.

LEARNING STYLE

Listen to teachers during professional development seminars, professional learning community (PLC) meetings, or other venues where pedagogy and best practices are discussed. You will likely hear them engage in conversations about teaching approaches that have dubious or no benefits to student learning. One of the more persistent zombie educational theories that refuses to die is to teach students according to their learning style. According to the American Psychological Association, "Previous surveys in the United States and other industrialized countries worldwide have shown that 80% to 95% of people believe in learning styles." First introduced by psychologist Walter Burke Barbe and his colleagues in the late 1970s, the theory posits that students learn best when they learn according to a particular learning modality. The three learning modalities are visual, kinesthetic/tactile, and auditory, popularly identified as VAK (Barbe, Swassing, Milone, 1979). Despite teachers' wide-held beliefs about student learning styles, there is no evidence to support the notion that correctly matching students to their learning modality results in increased student learning (Nancekivell, Shaw, & Gelman, 2019). All human brains learn equally well, whether it be from visual, auditory, or tactile input. As the Educational Endowment Foundation points out, "There is very limited evidence for any consistent set of learning 'styles' that can be used reliably to identify genuine differences in the learning needs of young people, and evidence suggests that it is unhelpful to assign learners to groups or categories on the basis of a supposed learning style." Even though the idea that students learn best when matched to a particular mode of delivery is not empirically sound, it can be helpful to present students with multiple means of representations.

TEACHING STRATEGY:

The Universal Design for Learning or UDL is a powerful brain-based learning framework proposed by Dr. David H. Rose of the Harvard Graduate School of Education. UDL is defined as the design and delivery of curriculum and instruction to meet the needs of all learners by providing them choices for what they are learning, why they are learning, and how they will share what they have learned. The framework suggests that students learn best when presented with three broad principles: multiple means of engagement or the "why" of learning;

multiple means of representation, the "what" of learning; and multiple means of action and expression, the "how" of learning (Murawski & Scott, 2019). Research suggests that the UDL framework is compelling for diverse students and students with disabilities because it increases engagement and provides learners access to the general education curriculum through flexible supports and scaffolding built into the lessons (Ok, Rao, Bryant, & McDougall, 2017). I use the UDL framework in various ways. I pay particular attention to providing my students with multiple representations of content. For example, when I teach the Declaration of Independence, I provide my students with the full text of the document. We then listen to a podcast in which the Declaration of Independence is read. We then examine a parchment reproduction of the Declaration of Independence to include Jefferson's rough draft. Finally, we examine a Dunlap broadside reproduction. I have found when I provide students with multiple representations of the Declaration of Independence, they are more likely to remember the main ideas and features of the document and generally seem more interested in their learning.

LEARNING PYRAMID

Another persistent but debunked educational theory is the learning pyramid. Although it is not clear who the progenitor of the theory is, many believe that it can be traced back to Edgar Dale and his Cone of Experience. The learning pyramid evolved from the cone in the early 1960s to the form we know today and has been perpetuated in staff development meetings and seminars ever since. The pyramid suggests that active learning is best for the long-term retention of learned content. That students learn in the following proportions:

- 10 percent of what they READ
- 20 percent of what they HEAR
- 30 percent of what they SEE
- 50 percent of what they SEE and HEAR
- 70 percent of what they SAY and WRITE
- 90 percent of what they DO

Educational psychologist Will Thalheimer explains, "People do not necessarily remember more of what they hear than what they read. They do not necessarily remember more of what they see and hear than what they see. The numbers are nonsense, and the order of potency is incorrect." The fallacy of this theory is that many teachers believe that active learning can only happen when students are doing something. Therefore, they will eschew approaches that require students to read, listen, and see in exchange for "hands-on" learning activities. And while learning by doing has been demonstrated to be a powerful learning tool, students must learn how to actively engage in other learning processes to be successful, self-directed learners. Active reading and listening are skills that can be taught, and it is crucial that students learn these critical skills.

▌ MASLOW'S HIERARCHY OF NEEDS

No education psychology course would be complete without an examination of Maslow's hierarchy of needs. First posited in 1943 by Abraham Maslow, the theory suggests that human motivation is predicated on meeting physiological needs, safety needs, love and belongingness, esteem needs, and self-actualization needs. The theory suggests that students must have their basic human survival needs met before they are motivated to higher levels of the hierarchy. These basic needs include food, water, shelter, clothes, safety, and security. Once these needs are satisfied, students must have their psychological needs met. These needs include love, belonging, friendship and closeness. The problem with Maslow's hierarchy is that Maslow never depicted his theory as a pyramid, never suggesting that the hierarchy was an inflexible, fixed series of progressions, or that each construct needed to be entirely fulfilled before progressing up the pyramid in a way that applied to everyone. Maslow wrote that human needs are relatively fluid and that a person may have many needs simultaneously. According to Maslow, "We have spoken so far as if this hierarchy was a fixed order, but actually, it is not nearly as rigid as we may have implied. It is true that most of the people with whom we have worked have seemed to have these basic needs in about the order that has been indicated. However, there have been a number of exceptions." And while most reasonable people would agree that it is difficult to learn while hungry or experiencing high levels of anxiety and stress, it is still possible to be creative, have intimate relationships, and feel accomplished under challenging situations. Additionally, Maslow's work has been criticized for its lack of scientific rigor and empirical evidence. One of the most frequently cited critiques of Maslow's work comes from researchers Wahaba and Bridgewell (1976). They point out that "The literature review shows that Maslow's Need Hierarchy Theory has received little clear or consistent support from the available research findings. Some of Maslow's propositions are rejected, while others receive mixed and questionable support at best." One of the reasons the hierarchy is not empirically supported is that his conclusions are difficult to replicate as he did not provide clear definitions for each need construct. Further, Maslow continued to add constructs to his theory throughout his lifetime.

In addition to the hierarchy not being based on empirical evidence, it has been criticized for being highly ethnocentric. With an almost exclusive bias toward White, college-educated men, the highest need for self-actualization is almost entirely concerned with individualistic needs such as self-esteem, achievement, and personal growth. Furthermore, Maslow did not consider gender, socioeconomic background, or the needs of collaborative cultures. In other words, Maslow's hierarchy of needs seems out of step with the highly diverse schools and students most teachers find themselves working with.

3.13 The Illusion of Knowing

In traditional and commonly accepted ways of learning, students spend countless hours in class being "filled up" with their teacher's knowledge and expertise, usually through direct methods such as lectures and demonstrations. After a unit of instruction, students are then assessed on how well they "learned" the material presented. In preparation for their assessment, the conventional approach is for students to review their reading and lecture notes. Many will highlight key concepts, vocabulary, and content, create flashcards, and engage in mass practice of the content. Additionally, many students will reread the textbook to make sure that they have not missed essential information. In this drill and practice scenario, one often finds students "cramming" as much information into their brains as they possibly can, usually days or even the night before the test. The reason why this approach is so persistent even though it does not yield long-term learning is that it creates an "illusion of knowing." In other words, students are not learning the material by tucking it away in long-term memory as much as they are becoming familiar with it in short-term memory after repeated exposure. Surface-level familiarity lulls the learner into a false sense of comprehension. Cramming may help a student pass a test, but the approach does not usually result in long-term learning, a deep understanding of concepts and applications, or transferability to other scenarios and situations.

A former student of mine named Juan best illustrates the illusion of knowing. Juan was a rock-star student in my eleventh-grade Advanced Placement U.S. history class several years ago. He was the kind of student every teacher dreams of having in their class. He was always prepared for class, reading and taking detailed notes from the textbook. And he consistently contributed to classroom discussions and activities and worked hard to do well on unit quizzes, exams, and written assessments like the document-based question. His efforts were rewarded, as he earned a five on the AP exam and an A in the course. Juan was a fantastic overall student and eventually received a scholarship to attend the Massachusetts Institute of Technology. A few years later, Juan came back to school to visit me. It was late April, and my students were frantically preparing for the AP test in an after-school study session. The students were quizzing one another in a rapid-fire game-show-style review. I suggested to Juan that he join us. Still, I warned the other students that Juan scored a 5 on the AP exam and would be a formidable opponent. The students sat in a circle, and the game show host peppered them with questions. When they got to Juan, they asked him to identify the Boston Massacre. Juan sat there with a subdued look on his face. Eventually, he shrugged his shoulders, indicating that he did not know the answer. Tricky question, after all, it has been a few years since he took the class, I thought to myself. I asked the host to ask Juan another question. "Name and describe three major New Deal agencies." Again, Juan sat there uncomfortably shaking his head, obviously unable to answer the question. After the game was over, I asked Juan what happened. He did so well in the class and scored a 5 on the exam. I thought for sure that he would breeze through the questions. Juan explained that he did well on the tests because he crammed a few days before. That as soon as the test was over, he forgot everything he "learned." This is the problem with the illusion of knowing.

TEACHING STRATEGY:

Retrieval practice is a learning strategy in which recalling information after instruction enhances and boosts learning. Retrieval practice is an excellent way to destroy the "illusion of knowing" by having students retrieve what they know about a topic, not what they think they know. The struggle to remember is what makes learning stick. As authors Brown, Roediger, and McDaniel (2014) point out, "Retrieval practice—recalling facts or concepts or events from memory—is a more effective learning strategy than review by rereading. Retrieval strengthens the memory and interrupts forgetting. A single, simple quiz after reading a text or hearing a lecture produces better learning and remembering than rereading the text or reviewing lecture notes" (p. 3). A recent meta-analysis of over fifty experiments analyzing the effects of retrieval practice found that the approach had a medium to large benefit in student learning (Agarwal, Nunes, & Blunt, 2021). A simple and effective way to include retrieval practice into daily lessons is to do a "knowledge check" after a lesson or instruction. For example, I like to have students perform a "brain dump" in which students brainstorm what they have learned by writing down everything they can recall about a lesson or reading passage. Sometimes I do this by having students create a graphic organizer such as a Venn diagram, concept map, or flowchart. On other occasions, it may be more appropriate to give students a quiz. Quizzes can be multiple-choice or short answers. Further, teachers can gamify retrieval practice by using online quizzing platforms such as Kahoot, Poll Everywhere, or Quizlet.

3.14 Action Research

Teachers have limited time with students, so it is essential that they use empirically based approaches that are supported by the research to maximize learning. An excellent way to make sure that students are learning as much as possible is for teachers to engage in action research. Action research is a process in which participants examine their educational practice systematically and carefully, using proven research techniques. It is based on the following assumptions:

- ⮑ Teachers work best on problems they have identified for themselves.
- ⮑ Teachers become more effective when encouraged to examine and assess their own work and then consider ways of working differently.
- ⮑ Teachers and administration help each other by working collaboratively.
- ⮑ Working with colleagues helps teachers and principals in their professional development (Watts, 1985).

Action research can be performed by an individual teacher, a small group of teachers, or throughout the entire school or district. Action research has several benefits, including building a better practitioner. When a teacher or group of teachers investigate a real-world problem or approach, they not only find solutions about what works and doesn't work in their situation, but they have an opportunity to build a professional culture. Action research elevates the profession, builds collegiality, and ultimately results in greater student learning. Action research is an iterative process of investigation. According to Eileen Ferrance (2000), action research consists of six phases of inquiry:

1. **Identification Of Problem Area**

    It is essential to limit the study's focus to one that is both purposeful and doable within the teacher's workspace. Further, the problem must be that teachers ultimately have power over or influence through their professional practice. Therefore, some sample study questions could be what changes in our teaching styles, curriculum design, materials, and professional support are needed to implement culturally responsive pedagogy? What classroom strategies are effective in developing student metacognition of their learning? What are student, teacher, and family perceptions of restorative justice practices?

2. **Collection and Organization Of Data**

    Select the most appropriate data for the problem being studied, keeping in mind the availability of the data. The more data points, the better. Researchers recommend using a minimum of three data points to achieve "triangulation" or the convergence point of multiple data sets. It is always a good idea to vary the sources of data. Data can be qualitative, which means that it is descriptive, such as interviews, open-ended surveys, and field observations. Or the data can be quantitative, which is data that can be measured. Some examples of quantitative data include test results, grades, attendance, checklists, and surveys.

3. **Interpretation of Data**

    Once the data has been collected, it must be interpreted to identify significant themes. Teachers must consider how the data can be viewed and shared with others and use tables, graphs, charts, or other visual representations.

4. **Action-Based on Data**

    At the heart of action research is using data to inform practice. Based on the data collected and the current literature on the problem, design a course of action, introduce a new teaching technique or other intervention to address the deficit. Make a change and study the results of the change. The research plan must manipulate a single variable so that resulting changes can be attributed to that variable. If several changes are made at once, it will be difficult to attribute the outcomes to the responsible variable. While implementing the new technique, continue to collect and study the data.

5. **Reflection**

   Critically analyze the data to determine if a positive change has occurred. If there was a change, teachers must be able to attribute the change to the intervention directly. Conversely, if no change was evident, it is essential to consider changes to practice to elicit the desired results.

6. **Next Steps**

   As a result of the action research, identify questions revealed by the data and additional action, revisions, and next steps.

3.15 Questions for Reflection

1. What are the three strategies for moving short-term memories into long-term memory? Describe each strategy and how they can be used in the education setting.

2. What is active learning? And what are some active learning strategies that teachers can use in their classroom?

3. How can an entrepreneurial mindset help students achieve success in and out of the classroom? How can teachers help students develop an entrepreneurial mindset?

4. What are some practical ways that edtech can help students achieve academically? Give specific examples.

5. What are some of the common myths about how we learn? Why have these myths remained so persistent?

6. What is the illusion of knowing? What are some methods teachers can use to help students learn deeply?

7. What is action research? And how can teachers use it to increase students' academic performance?

Chapter

04

**Classroom Culture for
21st Century Learning**

If kids come to us from strong, healthy functioning families, it makes our job easier. If they do not come to us from strong, healthy, functioning families, it makes our job more important.

—BARBARA COLOROSE

Great teachers focus not on compliance, but on connections and relationships.

—P.J. CAPOSEY

The strength of our student relationships makes the difference in translating our passion for teaching into their passion for learning.

—BETH MORROW

One of the cardinal rules of effective teaching is to "know your students." Knowledge of students is critical because a deep understanding of the individuals we teach is essential to forming positive relationships. According to William Powell and Ochan Kusuma-Powell in their book *How to Teach Now: Five Keys to Personalized Learning in the Global Classroom*, building positive relationships with students can do the following: create a psychologically safe environment for every learner, determine each student's readiness for learning, and identify multiple access points to the curriculum to increase engagement and success and develop and demonstrate greater emotional intelligence in the classroom. Since the average teacher spends over one thousand hours with their students in a typical school year, teachers' relationship is highly consequential.

When I first started teaching eleventh grade U.S. history many years ago, my primary focus was to be as knowledgeable as possible about my subject. I entered the profession in an alternative route to licensure program, having already earned an undergraduate degree in history, so I had a good foundation in my content when I started. However, I wanted to know more. I wanted to have command of my subject and learn as much as I possibly could. As a result, I spent countless hours in study. I read everything I could get my hands on, including historical monographs, popular history, articles, documentaries, websites, and anything else that would advance my knowledge of U.S. history. I took every opportunity to attend professional development workshops, seminars, and conferences. Additionally, I belonged to numerous professional organizations dedicated to the subject. Finally, in my zeal to be a content expert, I pursued a graduate degree in U.S. history. Indeed, my efforts paid off, as I was able to teach my subject confidently and with authority, so much so that I was selected to teach the U.S. History Advanced Placement course at my school. Because Advanced Placement courses are college-level classes, I thought of myself as an academic of sorts. In my pursuit of content mastery, I failed to consider that I was teaching students, not subjects. That is, developing a personal relationship with every student is one of the single most important things an educator can do to increase student learning. When students know that you care about them as individuals, they will be more inclined to put forth the effort and learn.

Developing strong relationships with learners can help teachers build a classroom culture based on trust and mutual respect. But solid relationships between the teacher and their students are only part of the equation. Teachers should help their students develop trusting relationships in the classroom by creating what is known as a community of learners. This psychologically safe atmosphere will allow students to take intellectual risks by removing obstacles like fear of chastisement or failure. Research indicates that strong teacher relationships are associated with short-term and long-term educational growth, such as greater student engagement, attendance, higher grades, fewer disruptive behaviors, and lower school dropout rates. Healthy relationships are beneficial to teachers as well. A study from the *European Journal of Psychology of Education* found that when teachers have strong relationships with their students, they tend to be happier and experience less stress and anxiety in the classroom.

Objectives:

- Educators will identify key aspects of adolescent development that will help students be academically, socially, and emotionally successful
- Understanding what teachers believe about their students
- Developing knowledge of students, family, and community
- Showing care, trust, and empathy
- Building a class culture and community of learners

4.1 Adolescent Development and Learning

A key component of building a positive classroom culture is understanding adolescent development. This is because a positive classroom culture is a critical component of the knowledge of students. Effective teachers realize that adolescence is a time of profound change and presents many challenges to the teacher, learner, and the learning environment. Research indicates that teens process information with their amygdala, unlike adults who cogitate using the brain's rational part called the prefrontal cortex. The amygdala, or "lizard brain," is where emotions are generated. The teenage brain does not fully develop until around twenty-five years of age, when connections between the prefrontal cortex and the amygdala fully form. Lack of brain development is why teenagers can be overly emotional and irrational leading to impulsive decisions and behavior. Therefore, teachers should take into account adolescent development when they are planning and implementing lessons.

Effective teachers consider their students' developmental needs to plan and implement learning activities that support their socio-emotional growth. As a child-rearing expert Dr. Ron Taffel points out, "Even as kids reach adolescence, they need more than ever for us to watch over them. Adolescence is not about letting go. It's about hanging on during a very bumpy ride." Adolescence is about self-discovery and forging an individual identity while cultivating membership in various social groups. Teens are trying to make sense of the world and their place in it. They are exploring fairness and justice. Teachers should provide students with opportunities to confront these issues in a supportive and safe environment.

TEACHING STRATEGY:

There are brain-based teaching strategies that teachers should use with adolescents. Using these approaches is important because teens are not little adults, nor are they children. Teachers must engage teens in developmentally appropriate learning strategies specifically designed to address their unique needs. For example, teachers should give straightforward directions and explanations while using multiple models of instruction. Because every student is unique and differs in how they perceive and comprehend information, teachers should provide students with various representations to communicate content. Additionally, teachers should help students develop competence in their discipline. Adolescence is an awkward time in which students do not want to feel incompetent or that people are judging them. Teachers can help students develop competence by knowing their students' strengths and weaknesses and help struggling students by offering extra help or tutoring. Finally, teachers should try to incorporate decision-making into their curriculum as much as possible. Teenagers' brains are rapidly developing in adolescence, and as a result, their decision-making processes are often flawed. Teachers should help their students evaluate potential solutions and think through consequences. An excellent teaching approach that allows students to think through various decisions and points of view is role-playing and simulations. For example, in a U.S. history class, students could recreate the constitutional convention and debate the critical issues of 1787, including slavery, representation, and federalism. Or students could put Harry Truman on trial for his decision to drop the atomic bomb on Hiroshima and Nagasaki. The possibilities are limitless. Role-play and simulations are an excellent opportunity for students to examine issues from various points of view and consider the pros and cons of historical decisions; however, a word of caution. Be sure that role-plays and simulations don't expose students to unnecessary trauma by engaging in hurtful or insensitive activities, especially for historically marginalized student populations.

4.2   Academic Supports for Young Learners

Students in most schools are grouped into grades by age and not ability. Unfortunately, this process overlooks the fact that students develop and mature at different rates. That is why teachers must provide sufficient support for developing learners to reach higher levels of understanding. The zone of proximal development (ZPD), first postulated by Russian psychologist Lev Vygotsky, refers to the difference between what a learner can do without help and what they can achieve with guidance and encouragement from a skilled partner. When students are in the ZPD, they are provided scaffolding or learning support from the teacher or a more knowledgeable peer to help them accomplish a task they could not do independently. ZPD is one reason collaborative learning is so effective, mainly when learners of mixed abilities are grouped together.

Further, collaborative learning supports socio-emotional learning by developing self-awareness, self-management, responsible decision-making, social awareness, and relational skills. All of which are critical skills as students grow and mature. Of course, for a teacher to effectively group students, educators must have deep knowledge of who their students are as learners. Instead of "flying blind" and making random instructional decisions based on conjecture, teachers should use data to drive instruction. Using multiple data points will help teachers make informed decisions that will elevate student learning and achievement. Some examples of data include:

- ⊃ Standardized test data from local, state, and national assessments
- ⊃ Teacher observations of student behavior and academic ability
- ⊃ Anecdotal information from students' teachers, counselors, coaches, and families
- ⊃ Knowledge of students' language skills through observation and assessment data
- ⊃ Knowledge of students' individual educational plan
- ⊃ Medical conditions including cognitive, emotional, and physical disabilities that may impact learning
- ⊃ Any other pertinent information that could impact student learning.

Knowledge of students can also mean understanding students' unique skills to include their strengths and weaknesses. Research conducted by the Center for Education Policy and Analysis at Stanford University reveals that knowledge of individual students' skills or KISS effectively increases student achievement for all learners. In addition, teachers who differentiate and target their instruction to meet their students' unique needs effect higher academic gains. According to Carol Ann Tomlinson, author, speaker, and differentiated instruction expert, "Differentiation is simply a teacher attending to the learning needs of a particular student or small groups of students, rather than teaching a class as though all individuals in it were basically alike."

4.3　What Teachers Believe about their Students: High Expectations, High Gains

What teachers believe about their students is instrumental to the success or failure of that student. Teachers' beliefs about their students are often self-fulfilling prophecies. In one of the first studies of the impact of the teacher's expectations on student achievement, Rosenthal and Jacobson (1968) demonstrated that positive expectations influence performance positively, while negative expectations do just the opposite, suggesting that "when we expect certain behaviors of others, we are likely to act in ways that make the expected behavior more likely to occur." Rosenthal and Jacobson called this phenomenon the Pygmalion effect after the character Pygmalion in Ovid's epic poem *Metamorphoses*. In the story, the sculptor Pygmalion fell in love with a statue that he created. The Pygmalion effect simply stated is a self-fulling prophecy. In other words, how you treat someone has a direct impact on that person's behavior. As it applies to teaching, when teachers have high expectations for student performance, students will rise to the occasion and work hard to fulfill the expectation. The reverse is also true. When teachers believe that students are not capable of learning, they usually do not.

What teachers believe about their student's capacity to do high-level work impacts the teacher's expectations and behavior; when teachers believe that their students can achieve, they are more likely to engage in teaching moves and interactions that will improve student achievement (Mellom, Straubhaar, Balderas, Ariail, & Portes, 2018). To combat what President George W. Bush called the "soft bigotry of low expectations," teachers should become "warm demanders" of all students. According to education researcher and author Lisa Delpit, a warm demander is a teacher who "expect a great deal of their students, convince them of their brilliance, and help them to reach their potential in a disciplined and structured environment." It is amazing how students will rise, or sink, to meet their teachers' expectations. Teachers who erroneously believe their students cannot learn or come from cultures that don't appreciate education only perpetuate negative stereotypes. Teachers must make high expectations an integral component of their classroom culture and demand that all students rise to the occasion.

Having high expectations is easier to do when teachers maintain a structured learning environment. As much as students may resist procedure and protocol, they crave the predictability that structure it provides. This is especially true of students whose lives are scarred by the trauma of poverty, neighborhood and family violence, and systemic racism. Classroom discipline is less about individual behaviors and consequences and more about managing classroom processes. When students from affluent backgrounds become disengaged in school, they usually have ample opportunities to regain what they have lost through tutoring, enrichment activities, and other second chances. When students from high-poverty areas fall behind, there is no safety net to help them turn things around. As a result, these students experience higher dropout rates, higher unemployment, higher poverty rates, poor health, and involvement with the criminal justice system (National Research Council, 2004). There are no second chances for these students. That is why it is crucial to get it right the first time and warmly demand all students' academic success. Students will rise to the challenge when pushed by someone who genuinely and sincerely cares about them.

4.4 Knowledge of Students and Students' Culture

Most teachers want to see their students succeed, but they may not know the best approach to reach diverse learners. As a result, a cultural "disconnect" may be preventing them from being effective teachers (McKoy, MacLeod, Walter, & Nolker, 2017). Research indicates that preservice educators' knowledge of diverse cultures was "marginal." These teachers usually displayed aspects of students' surface culture, such as celebrating ethnic holidays, foods, and music. Some teachers erroneously think that teaching all students the same without regard to culture is equitable. Many teachers claim to be "color-blind," but this notion easily conceals entrenched racial ideas that have resulted in persistent discrimination. Instead of denying that entrenched and institutionalized racism exists, teachers should become "color-conscious" and use students' culture as a way to build bridges and relationships with their students. Many teachers do not consider their students' unique cultures when they teach because they believe that good teaching is transcendent. It is identical for all students regardless of backgrounds, settings, and circumstances (Gay, 2010).

Culture does matter. It is the foundation from which all education is built. Teaching through a cultural lens helps teachers understand the lived experiences of their students. By utilizing students' unique cultural backgrounds, culturally competent teachers give voice to students who have been historically marginalized by giving them a space to feel a sense of dignity through social, linguistic, and cultural expressions (Gay, 2010). The Center for Advanced Research on Language Acquisition defines culture as "the shared patterns of behaviors and interactions, cognitive constructs, and affective understanding that are learned through a process of socialization." These shared patterns identify the members of a cultural group while also distinguishing those of another group. Zaretta Hammond, in her book *Culturally Responsive Teaching & The Brain: Promoting Authentic Engagement and Rigor Among Culturally and Linguistically Diverse Students,* points out that culture is composed of three layers; namely, surface culture, shallow culture, and deep culture. Surface culture is the detectable level of culture to include food, music, holidays, dance, and fashion, to name a few aspects. Most teachers and schools operate at this level of culture, as demonstrated by Black History Month, National Hispanic American Heritage Month, and Asian Pacific American Heritage Month. Shallow culture consists of the unspoken rules concerning daily interactions and norms, including courtesy, attitudes toward elders, family, friends, and so on. Other aspects of shallow culture include nonverbals, such as eye contact, personal space, and appropriate touching. Deep culture deals with feelings and attitudes that we learn by being members of a particular group. It involves differences primarily from a person's conscious awareness. It is often taken for granted, such as assumptions, expectations, attitudes, and values that make up our worldviews and behaviors. Deep culture informs our relationships, perceptions of time, spirituality, and problem-solving. A commonly used analogy to describe the differences between the three types of culture is the iceberg. The smallest part of the iceberg visible above the water line is the surface culture in this analogy. The iceberg just beneath the water's surface represents shallow culture. In contrast, the part of the iceberg that is entirely out of view represents deep culture.

WHY TEACHERS' KNOWLEDGE OF STUDENTS' FAMILIES IS IMPORTANT FOR STUDENT SUCCESS

In addition to knowledge of students, teachers must also know their students' families. Educators should see their students' families as important cultural and intellectual assets. When properly utilized, understanding students' families can positively impact student achievement by building an encouraging, inclusive school culture welcoming to all. In other words, teachers should see their students' families as an ally and an asset rather than a liability. I use the term families instead of parents because the word family is more inclusive and covers the range of adults who may care for children beyond a child's biological parents. For example, modern family structures may include single parents, same-sex couples, extended families, and grandparent families. A tweet from Professor Sirry Alang (@ProfAlang) that went viral during the COVID-19 quarantine and subsequent distance learning illustrates this. She tweeted, "Teachers, ur class convos are broadcasted in everyone's homes. The # of times the teacher has said 'your mom and dad' to my kid's class is infuriating. But a BRAVE kid just said ... 'But I only told my grandma at lunchtime because my sister and I live with our grandma.'" Over forty years of research suggests that when families are involved in their student's education, attendance improves, there are higher math and reading proficiency scores, better social skills displayed, fewer discipline referrals and placements in special education, and higher graduation rates and matriculation to higher education (Kaplan & Owings, 2015).

Between 2000 and 2017, the percentage of White public-school children dropped from 61 to 48 percent, according to the National Center for Education Statistics. However, the teaching field has remained relatively unchanged, with 79 percent of its teachers being White, 9 percent Latinx, 7 percent Black, and only 2 percent Asian (Taie & Westat, 2020). Most teachers reflect the dominant culture's mores and bring perspectives shaped by their White, female, middle-class, monolingual experiences into the classroom. As a result, teachers may have difficulty relating to families different from their own. Because they see the world through the lens of their own experience, they may erroneously decode minority families' actions and behaviors in negative ways. "These parents don't value education" is a sad refrain from many teachers who don't understand that many barriers prevent diverse families from participating in their child's education. For example, educators may interpret a parent's inability to be involved in their student's schooling as a lack of interest or erroneously believe that education is not a priority for them. Instead, socioeconomic factors may require parents to work two, three, or even more jobs. Their shifts may be at odds with the typical school day schedule, as they may have to work swing or graveyard shifts, making it challenging to participate in their child's classroom and afterschool activities. Often, parents have more than one school-age child, exacerbating challenges of parents' time and energy. Some families may not have reliable transportation to get to their child's school. Others may be discouraged from participating at school because of past negative experiences, feelings of intimidation and exclusion due to language challenges, or differences in cultural norms. For example, in many cultures, teachers are highly respected and are not questioned by students or their families. This cultural norm may lead to families taking a hands-off approach to their children's schooling, which some teachers could interpret as apathy. This is true of many immigrant families because they may not understand the social expectations of parental involvement at their child's school. Meeting families where they are is essential in developing school family engagement. Teachers and school leaders must change their perspectives of families and see them through a strength-based lens instead of a deficit-based lens. Teachers should not look at their students and their families as people who need to be rescued or saved from their terrible circumstances. In other words, teachers must resist the urge to engage in the "savior complex." As well-intentioned as teachers may be, it exploits the power differential between educators, students, and their families. Families need allies, not saviors.

In her book *Beyond the Bake Sale,* Harvard Graduate School of Education professor Dr. Karen L Mapp points out that there are four core beliefs that educators should use as a foundation for engaging families. The first is that all parents have dreams for their children and want the best for them. Teachers should recognize that not all parents express this trait the same way. Families may have different priorities as they face structural problems such as poverty and mental and physical health issues. Still, they all have dreams and aspirations for their children. Second, teachers should see parents as teaching allies to support their children's learning and growth. Teachers can do this by inventorying the strengths and assets that families bring to the school, including their students' knowledge. One of the most powerful tools in the teacher's tool bag is understanding who their students are. Families can provide a treasure trove of information regarding their learning habits, their interests, their favorite subjects, and pastimes, as well as their trauma and challenges.

PARENTS AND SCHOOL STAFF SHOULD BE EQUAL PARTNERS IN THE EDUCATION OF STUDENTS

Dr. Mapp uses American football as an analogy for this concept. She explains that in football, a team is composed of an offensive squad and a defensive squad. The offense's job is to run and pass the ball down the field to score touchdowns. The defense's job is to stop their opponent from doing the same. Both squads are equally important in winning games. This is true of educators and families. Both are on the same team, and both must respect the knowledge and skills that each brings from their own experiences, even though they each have different roles to play. A simple thing teachers can do to communicate with families effectively is to make school communication less jargon-laden and authoritarian, whether written, spoken, or online. This type of communication can cause confusion and alienation with families and may lead them to disengage. Finally, Dr. Mapp points out that the responsibility for cultivating and sustaining partnerships among school, home, and community rests primarily with school staff. There is a hierarchy between school staff and families in most schools, reflecting historical racial, class, and educational levels and divisions. School staff must be willing to reach out and break through these existing barriers. Educators must be persistent in their efforts, as many families have been historically shut out of school and may need time to build confidence and trust. Teachers must be relentless in their efforts to demonstrate that they authentically want to partner with families and genuinely care about their children.

4.5   Knowledge of Students' Community

In addition to engaging with students' families, teachers must know the communities they serve. When schools lack significant connections to the neighborhood, the community may perceive the school as being unwelcoming and aloof. To make schools more inviting and approachable, educators must understand the community's story by knowing who lives in the community. One of the first steps teachers can take to know their communities is understanding the neighborhood's demographics. Demographic information may include nationalities, age distributions, political and religious affiliations, socioeconomic data such as income levels, occupations, living status (homeowner or renter), languages spoken, and education levels. In addition, knowledge of community means knowing the community's history, institutions, and influential community members past and present and local businesses operating in the area.

Since most teachers do not live where they teach, they should make an effort to get out into the community as often as possible to meet students, families, and neighbors where they are. Teachers can do this by occasionally walking with their students to and from school. Walking with students is a great way to understand the neighborhood better, get up close and personal, and get to know the students one-on-one. Additionally, teachers could patron local businesses, houses of worship or attend local celebrations and institutions such as libraries, museums, and cultural centers. Some schools have successfully done home visits to get to know their students, families, and communities. Meeting families allows them to remain in their comfort zones, develops closer partnerships and positive communication, and helps create a support network for students and their families. In addition, teacher home visits have been associated with student achievement. The research revealed that schools with strong home visit programs had higher rates of students regularly attending school and passing scores on state standardized English language, arts, and math tests.

In many communities, public schools do more than just educate neighborhood kids. They are cultural institutions that help build relationships and transmit a community's shared memory. An excellent example of how a school can help build community is the Crestwood Elementary School Community Garden in Las Vegas, Nevada. Founded by Juliana Urtubey, a teacher at the school and the 2020 National Teacher of the Year, the garden has been incredibly successful in building bridges between the students' home life and their school. Urtubey, an immigrant herself, built upon her past experiences as a newcomer and understands the importance of bringing together the mostly White teaching staff with the surrounding Latinx community. The garden provides a space where parents and teachers can come together as equals through community participation days, breaking down cultural and linguistic barriers commonly found in more institutional settings such as parent-teacher conferences. A school garden is a place where friendships blossom and relationships grow. The students benefit when they learn the knowledge and skills necessary to produce a variety of fruits and vegetables in addition to valuable STEAM skills. Further, outdoor seating transformed the garden into an open-air classroom, complete with decorative murals painted by local artists celebrating ethnobotanical planting and cultural pride.

4.6   Care, Trust, and Empathy for Student Success

As the old saying goes, "Students don't care how much you know until they know how much you care." Caring for students can be seen in teachers' attitudes, values, and beliefs about students expressed both verbally and nonverbally. In other words, caring is a "point of convergence" between what the teacher believes and how teachers interact with students in the classroom (Jensen, Whiting, & Chapman, 2018). Caring for students means honoring them as human beings, having positive interactions with them, and setting high expectations for behavior and academic performance. Showing students that you care can yield huge dividends. For example, studies indicate that students who have had positive relationships with their teachers in high school experience higher confidence levels, are less likely to drop out of school, and are generally more confident about their chances for gainful employment after high school.

There are several things that teachers can do to build a culture of caring in their classrooms. One of the most important is to build trust with learners. To build trust, teachers should engage in a pedagogy of listening. Nothing says "I care about you" more than taking a genuine interest in what students have to say. And since 70 percent of communication is nonverbal, it is equally important to demonstrate that teachers actively listen and are present through their body language. Teachers are incredibly busy people, and most have become experts at multitasking several different duties at once. But giving students 100 percent of your attention will go a long way at developing trust, rapport, and building positive relationships with students. I remember early in my career, my students would come up to my desk eager to share something significant that happened in their lives, usually at the worst possible moment as I was frantically trying to input grades, take attendance, answer emails, or some other similar task. I got good at going through the motions, as I appeared to be "listening" by nodding my head, occasionally looking up from what I was doing, and mumbling, "Oh, wow, no kidding?" or some other generic affirmation. I soon realized, however, that I hadn't heard a word they said. So now, I stop what I am doing to give my students my undivided attention. And when I cannot do that, I explain to them that I have something important I must finish, but that as soon as I am done, I would love to hear what they have to tell me. Better yet, I ask them to swing by after school, or some other quiet time, so that I can give them my full undivided attention.

According to Zaretta Hammond (2010), teachers should be sensitive to the emotions and feelings behind the words students use, suspend judgment, and listen to students with compassion. Unfortunately, regardless of culture, many young people don't have the experience, skills, or knowledge to communicate with adults effectively. That is why teachers must meet students where they are and recognize and value their cultural way of communicating.

To build trusting and caring relationships with students, teachers need to establish rapport to affirm their students' unique cultures and identities. One of the easiest but overlooked ways to do this is to learn students' names and pronounce them correctly. Sometimes it takes me a while to do this, but names are important. It is how we are identified in the world. It is OK to ask students for help in pronouncing their name, but it may be beneficial to do this before or after class not to put the student "on the spot." Teachers should make every effort to make students feel welcome and appreciated. Building rapport means that teachers should try and connect with students on a personal level. Teachers can do this by engaging students with small talk to learn about their interests. I like to arrive at class early and leave late to have plenty of opportunities to talk with students informally, one-on-one. As motivational guru Tony Robbins says, "Energy flows where attention goes." Stand in the hallway during passing period and greet students as they enter the classroom. Rituals like this is an excellent way to start the day, and it signals to students that you take a personal interest in their well-being. Let students see you outside of the classroom. Doing so reminds students that you are an actual person. Go to students' sporting events, chaperone dances, and school activities. Especially those that celebrate cultural heritage. Nothing says "I care" more than spending time with someone. To build rapport, teachers should be their authentic selves. Don't try and be someone you are not. Students can see through this a mile away. Let students know about your interests and hobbies, even if they are corny. I have a display case in my classroom where I like to keep my collection of historically themed toys. I have Funko Pops, bobbleheads, and Barbie dolls depicting Benjamin Franklin, Rosa Parks, and Abraham Lincoln. I know it's weird for a grown man to play with dolls (action figures), but don't be afraid to be vulnerable, as uncomfortable as it is sometimes.

▌EMPATHY

Showing students empathy is another way in which teachers can build positive relationships with their students. Empathy is the ability to step into another persons' shoes, with the desire to understand their feelings, points of view, and lived experiences. Empathetic teachers will then use their knowledge of students to guide their interactions and teaching. Empathy can be broken down into two main categories; namely empathic concern and empathetic perspective-taking. Empathic concern is when a teacher feels sympathy and compassion for their students. Empathetic perspective-taking is applying empathy when dealing with others. This enables teachers to develop students' knowledge by helping teachers connect with their students on an individual and personal basis. Teachers who demonstrate an understanding of their students as individuals may connect with them more effectively, forming relationships that could translate into higher student achievement. For example, a recent study of seventh- and eighth-grade Latinx students revealed that authentically caring relationships are the foundation of academic achievement. In addition to academic instruction, interpersonal relationships are an integral component of student learning (Newcomer, 2018). The empathetic teacher can understand their classroom from the students' perspective. In other words, empathetic teachers demonstrate their cultural awareness through their actions, such as choice of curriculum, pedagogical decisions, and language choices.

Teachers who fail to develop robust knowledge of students, to include empathy, may produce a variety of negative consequences such as unnecessary remediation, excessive discipline, and equating the students' disruptive behavior and low academic performance to defects in the child's home life and community (Williams, Edwards, Kuhel, & Lim, 2016). In a study of eighteen educators, Peck, Maude, and Brotherson (2015) found that empathetic teachers embrace inclusion, are responsive to student and families' needs, accept and respond to students' cultures, and engage students and families in meaningful conversations. However, as Maya Angelou points out, "I think we all have empathy. We may not have enough courage to display it." Building a culture of caring based on trust and empathy takes time. Teachers must deliberate about cultivating relationships that will translate into student achievement in their limited time, as forty-year veteran educator Rita Pierson explains in her TED talk, "Every Kid Needs a Champion," "Kids don't learn from people they don't like."

4.7   School Climate and Culture to Build a Community of Learners

A positive school climate and culture are fundamental components to high teaching and learning levels because they set the stage for achievement. As Harvard education professor Roland Barth points out, in schools with healthy climates and cultures, students and staff are genuinely engaged, have better attendance, higher student achievement, and have fewer disciplinary problems. "A school's culture has more influence on life and learning in the schoolhouse than the president of the country, the state department of education, the superintendent, the school board, or even the principal, teachers, and parents can ever have." For this reason, building a strong school climate and culture is crucial in providing a 21st-century education.

Frequently the words *school climate and culture* are used interchangeably in describing the school's milieu. However, they mean different things. School climate is challenging to define because it can mean different things to different people. Still, according to Freiberg and Stein (1999), school climate is "the heart and soul of the school." The climate causes students and teachers to engage in the school and want to attend with pride. It results from policies and actions put in place by principals and teachers and describes a school's "feel." The National School Climate Center points out that climate is based on the patterns of people's school life experiences; it reflects the norms, goals, values, interpersonal relationships, teaching, learning and leadership practices, and organizational structures that comprise school life (2009). In other words, a school's climate is what makes students and teachers eager to come to school. It is the emotional tone set by the principal and teachers. It helps students feel socially, emotionally, and physically safe in schools. Often the school's climate is taken for granted. Still, as best-selling author, educational leadership, and school climate expert Peter Dewitt explains, "There are people who will say 'We don't have time for school climate because we have so much on our plate.' And my philosophy is school climate is the plate that everything else has to go on."

School culture refers to a school's unique persona. It's that feeling one gets when walking into a school and knowing that something special is happening there. According to education reformer Michael Fullan (2007), "School culture may be defined as the guiding beliefs and expectations evident in the way a school operates." In other words, school culture is the way things get done in a school. It is an enduring pattern of meaning and practice that profoundly affects faculty and staff attitudes and approaches. A helpful way to think about positive school culture is to consider what it is not. A school's culture often operates under the conscious awareness of students and staff. Hence, a school's culture is durable and long-lasting, unlike climate. In the book *Shaping School Culture: The Heart of Leadership*, authors Terrence Deal and Kent Peterson point out, "School cultures are complex webs of traditions and rituals that have been built up over time as teachers, students, parents, and administrators work together and deal with crises and accomplishments. As a result, cultural patterns are highly enduring, have a powerful impact on performance, and shape the ways people think, act and feel."

School culture is built with all school staff members' contributions, including the administration, teachers, support staff, parents, and the greater community. As the African proverb states, "It takes a village to raise a child." According to Bill Dagett, founder of the International Center for Leadership in Education, school culture matters. When Dagett analyzed the top-performing schools in America, he found that the top 1 percent of the highest performing schools had one thing in common, a positive school culture. A recent study indicates that when teachers build a safe and supportive school and classroom cultures that engage all learners, they facilitate their students' academic success and social and emotional well-being (Ohlson, Swanson, Adams-Manning, & Byrd, 2016). Negative or "toxic" cultures do just the opposite. They are characterized by, among other things, a school staff that is fragmented, frustrated, and feels a sense of hopelessness. A school in which serving students' needs has become a secondary consideration to adults' needs and wants.

Just as schools have climates and cultures, individual classrooms do too. And it is just as important, if not more so, for teachers to build and maintain a positive environment from which all students can learn. Research indicates that children thrive in classrooms when teachers expect all students to contribute and where everyone is valued. There are several ways that teachers can build positive classroom cultures. The most important is for teachers to develop positive relationships with their students. All students should feel safe, connected, and engaged at school. For example, a study of behaviorally at-risk African American students indicated that when teachers built supportive relationships with their students, there were measurable increases in the students' positive social outcomes and overall academic achievement (Decker, Dona, & Christenson, 2007). Unfortunately, building strong relationships, especially with marginalized populations, is not always achieved. A study conducted by the EdWeek Research Center indicated that teachers believe almost a third of marginalized students feel very or somewhat uncomfortable at their school, at 29 percent for Black students, 34 percent for LGBTQ students, 29 percent for immigrant students, and 26 percent for students from low-income families.

Strong teacher-student relationships can reduce students' feelings of isolation and alienation and help them build resilience to cope with childhood trauma. John Hattie, in his book *Visible Learning: A Synthesis of Over 800 Meta-Analyses Relating to Achievement*, writes that "Having teachers who care, that take time to listen, possess empathy, and demonstrate a positive regard for others, have a greater impact on student achievement than those who do not" (Hattie, 2010, p. 118). Additionally, teachers should facilitate positive relationships between students. One way to do this is to have clear, consistent, and mutually agreed-upon classroom rules and procedures. Students crave structure and predictability despite their protestations to the contrary. When teachers manage classrooms well and are on task, students have fewer opportunities to engage in disruptive behaviors. As the old saying goes, "Idle hands are the devil's workshop." Just like adults, when students respect and adhere to social norms and expectations, they are more likely to live and work together in harmony.

It is crucial to build strong relationships with students and between students. It is equally important to foster positive collaborative relationships with their families and communities. In other words, teachers should invite input from various stakeholders in making assorted decisions that impact the classroom, such as curriculum, instruction, enrichment activities, resources, celebrations, and recognitions. Teachers can do this by maintaining open lines of communication through digital technologies such as creating a classroom website, emails, digital newsletters, and social media posts. It is essential to meet stakeholders where they are, understanding that not every family has access to the Internet and should employ traditional communication methods such as phone calls, handbills, and snail mail when appropriate. Additionally, teachers should consider parents' work schedules and the primary language spoken because it is crucial to make all family members feel included and appreciated. Not everyone has the luxury of working "banker's hours," and teachers must be flexible in meeting all families' needs.

Another thing teachers can do to build positive classroom climates and cultures is to have high expectations of all students. Student achievement is a self-fulfilling prophecy. When teachers sincerely believe their students can achieve academic success, they usually do (more on this later). Celebrate accomplishments by offering praise and recognition that is specific and genuine. Blanket statements like "good job" or "well done" spoken to the class are not enough. Target individual students for compliments and be descriptive of the exact behavior that warrants the recognition. For example, "Rosa, I enjoyed reading your essay. Your research and writing have improved dramatically since the beginning of the years." Better yet, teach students to praise one another when they experience success. Soon the classroom will be overflowing with positive vibes. Similarly, maintain a clean and organized classroom that reflects the diversity of the students who learn there. Research indicates that the symbolic environment, such as wall color and decor, and objects displayed in the classroom powerfully affect classroom culture (Cheryan, Ziegler, Plaut, & Meltzoff, 2014). Maintain a positive attitude, even during difficult times. As best-selling author Jeff Keller points out, "attitude is everything," and students are watching how you handle difficult or tense situations. Using humor is an excellent way to deal with challenging circumstances or frustration. Don't take yourself too seriously. Abraham Lincoln was famous for his self-deprecating humor. For example, during one of his debates with Stephen Douglas for the U.S. Senate seat in Illinois in 1858, Douglas accused Lincoln of being two-faced. Lincoln calmly retorted to the amusement of the crowd, "I leave it to my audience: If I had two faces, would I be wearing this one?"

▍COMMUNITY OF LEARNERS

When teachers build positive classroom climates and cultures based on personal relationships with high expectations for student learning, they create a community of learners. A community of learners can be defined as "a group of people who share values and beliefs and who actively engage in learning from one another—learners from teachers, teachers from learners, and learners from learners. They thus create a learning-centered environment in which students and educators are actively and intentionally constructing knowledge together." (Learning and the Adolescent Mind, p. 1). In other words, learning is more than individual sense-making. Deep and meaningful learning occurs when students build collective knowledge through a social process consistent with constructivist learning theory. The benefit of a classroom of a community of learners is that it satisfies all students' basic desire to be included. According to research, a sense of belonging can increase student academic performance, as "a student's subjective sense of belonging appears to have a significant impact on several measures of motivation and engagement and persistent effort in difficult academic work" (Goodenow, 1992, p. 15). When students come together to accomplish a common goal, they form and maintain positive relationships while having the opportunity to hone social skills such as collaboration, communication, and shared responsibility by helping one another and learning from each other. Additionally, when students are members of a community of learners, they feel empowered to take intellectual risks by asking questions, expressing unpopular opinions, playing devil's advocate, and publicly debating controversial ideas safely and respectfully. According to a study of 11,794 sixteen-year-olds in 830 high schools, when students think of their school as a community of learners rather than as a top-down bureaucracy, they are more likely to experience gains in engagement and achievement (Lee & Smith, 1995).

TEACHING STRATEGY:

There are several things a teacher can do to build a community of learners in their classroom. However, one of the most important steps a teacher can take is to be a role model to students by demonstrating the behavior they wish to see in their students. Teachers are ostensibly preparing their students to become productive members of society. Therefore, they must equip them with the skills and dispositions that will help them be successful. For example, I believe that it is vital that students become lifelong learners. This is because, as Albert Einstein famously quipped, "The more I learn, the more I realize how much I don't know." Therefore, it is impossible to teach students everything they need to know in school to succeed. Instead, students need to become lifelong learners to make sense of their world, prepare for more and better opportunities, and improve their overall quality of life. I demonstrate this principle by sharing with my students what I am currently reading. I want them to know that I constantly learn new things even though I am an educated person. Additionally, I tell my students about visits to museums, historical sites, libraries, college campuses, and other places of learning.

Another way a teacher can model what it means to be a member of a community of learners is to engage with students and adults positively and constructively. Students must see that people may disagree with one another in these divided times but remain respectful and civil. One can argue that analyzing an issue from multiple perspectives is integral to the proper functioning of a democratic republic and should be modeled in the classroom. Disallowing divergent points of view is anathema to the free exchange of ideas necessary for innovation and intellectual development. In a biography of the 18th-century French philosopher Voltaire, Evelyn Beatrice Hall captured the free-expression zeitgeist when she wrote, "I don't agree with what you said, but I will defend to the death your right to say it." One of the ways to facilitate the free exchange of ideas in the classroom is to teach students to avoid ad hominem attacks. In other words, argue against a speaker's ideas or position, not against the speaker personally. To do this effectively, the teacher must establish norms of behavior and conduct. Norms are similar to class rules in that they govern how students are to behave but differ in that norms are "an agreement among members of a classroom or school about how they will treat one another," according to Gary Borich, professor of educational psychology at The University of Texas at Austin. The teacher usually develops classroom rules at the beginning of the school year. The students create norms once school has begun. With the teacher's help, students can address norms that pertain to how students treat one another, especially as it relates to learning. Norms may include building trust between students as they ask their questions, become independent learners, address controversial or sensitive topics, support one another to take intellectual risks and demonstrate vulnerability as they reveal aspects of their personal lived experience.

4.8 Teaching Students to ask their Own Questions

In most high school classrooms, teachers do most of the talking. A study of student engagement revealed that, on average, teachers talk between 70 and 80 percent of the time in the upper grades, using teaching methods such as direct instruction, demonstrations, and asking students questions. Even the somewhat interactive Q & A process is dominated by teacher talk as teachers usually follow a discernable pattern where the teacher initiates a question, the students respond, and the teacher evaluates the response and usually builds upon it with detailed explanations. This pattern of classroom talk that consists of initiation, response, and evaluation is sometimes referred to as IRE and is the cornerstone of most classroom dialogue (Meehan, 1979). Further, teacher talk increases as students progress through the grades and academic content becomes more specialized. Thus, by the time students enroll in college, the lecture approach becomes the de facto method of disseminating knowledge. The question then becomes, when teachers talk, who is doing the thinking? In other words, in many classrooms, teachers bear most of the cognitive load, allowing students to be passive recipients of the teacher's instruction. However, this is beginning to change as university faculty and K–12 teachers realize that direct instruction in many situations results in poor academic performance and achievement compared with active learning strategies. For example, a meta-analysis of 225 studies indicates that when professors utilize passive learning strategies such as lectures in undergraduate STEM classes, failure rates increase by 55 percent. Further, when university faculty used active approaches to teaching and learning, there were better overall grades and a 36 percent drop in class failure rates (Freeman et al., 2014). And according to a feature published in *Harvard Magazine*, university professors who engage in "active learning" strategies may be beginning to outnumber those that prefer direct instruction or the lectio approach that has been utilized in the halls of higher learning for over six hundred years. This trend will continue as older professors with more traditional techniques retire and are replaced by younger ones who hold more progressive views of teaching and learning.

An excellent strategy to get students actively engaged in their learning is to teach them to ask their own questions. When students are taught to ask their own questions, they become active participants in their learning. Further, they are building a community of learners, which results in high cognitive demand, student agency, and growing students into independent thinkers and learners. For example, research suggests that when students are asked to generate questions at the beginning of a unit of study, they are likely to ask a question that comes from a genuine interest to understand and focus on a topic they care about (Scardamalia & Bereiter, 1992). Teachers can then leverage this knowledge of students into effective instruction that is both personal and relevant to the learner.

TEACHING STRATEGY:

In his best-selling book *The Global Achievement Gap*, Harvard University professor of education Tony Wagner interviewed numerous CEOs about the essential qualities they looked for in prospective employees. One key trait that came up repeatedly was workers' ability to ask good questions. As Wagner put it, "Problem-posing is more important than problem-solving." This makes sense in a world where almost everyone has instant access to information through the Internet and related technologies. As a result, agency is no longer being able to recall or even locate the correct answer. Instead, actual worth comes from creating new knowledge and ideas by asking good questions. There are three things that teachers can do to get their students to ask good questions.

1.   Building a Community of Learners

As discussed, the teacher's primary goal is to create a classroom community in which student questions are expected. Further, students must have a supportive environment to learn so that students feel encouraged to take intellectual risks free from ridicule. In other words, students must feel emotionally safe to make mistakes and be vulnerable.

2. **Develop Students' Questioning Skills by Providing Students with Questioning Stems.**

   These stems could be displayed on the classroom walls, as handouts, or posted on a class website or learning management system. Teachers should model for their students how to use the stems throughout a lesson. Some popular question stems include Why is ...? Why did ...? How might ...? How did ...? Who should ...? When might ...? What if ...? Predict ...? Why do you think ...? Where might ...? In what ways ...? What do you think about ...? Why do you agree/disagree ...? What advice would you give ...? What would happen if ...? What caused ...? What are the pros and cons of ...? Do you agree that ...? Explain.

3. **Question Evaluation Checklist**

   Providing students with a protocol to evaluate their questions is an excellent strategy to generate good questions that pertain to the lesson at hand. Questions include:

   ⮑ Is it connected to the topic?

   ⮑ Is the question open-ended?

   ⮑ Is the question straightforward?

   ⮑ Does it promote student thinking?

4. **Make Student Questions a Part of Every Lesson**

   There are a variety of techniques and approaches that are excellent ways to prompt students to ask their own questions. The key here is to be intentional by providing students with time. Some popular strategies are:

   Think-Pair-Share - This is a classic teaching strategy in which the teacher poses a question to the class. The students are then given time to think about their responses individually and share their ideas with a neighbor. For purposes of generating questions, students could pose a question to their shoulder buddy using the questioning stems previously mentioned.

   ⮑ 10 by 10 – In this activity, teachers give students 10 minutes to generate 10 questions. This can be done individually or in small groups. Have students implement the question evaluation checklist for each question to ensure high-quality questions.

➲ Visual & Aural Prompt – Provide students with a visual or auditory cue such as a picture, painting, illustration, political cartoon, video clip, song, or speech that in some way relates to the topic of the lesson. Have students generate questions in response to what they see or hear.

4.9 Questions for Reflection

1. Explain why it is important to understand how adolescents develop intellectually, socially and emotionally to provide the best education possible. Give some specific examples.

2. Why are high expectations for all learners an important component of student achievement?

3. How can teachers use knowledge of their students' families, community, and culture to increase student achievement?

4. What are some strategies educators can use to get to know their students?

5. Why is school climate and culture important to student academic success? How can educators build effective positive climates and cultures in their classrooms and schools?

6. What is a community of learners? And how do they contribute to student academic achievement? How can an educator build a community of learners in their school?

7. What is the benefit of students asking their own questions? What are some strategies to get students to ask their own questions?

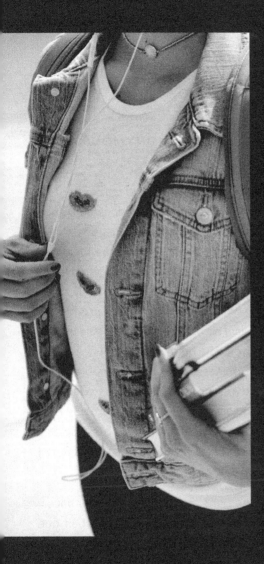

Chapter

05

**Culturally Responsive
Teaching and Social-Emotional
Learning for the 21st Century**

Equal is everyone getting the same thing. Fair is everyone getting what they need to be successful. We will always try to be fair, but it won't always feel equal.

—ANONYMOUS

The Jeffersonian ideal that "all men are created equal" is a cornerstone of our national creed. And while his declaration was more pronouncement than fact, it has served as a lofty goal for which we, as a nation, continue to strive. For example, the modern Civil Rights Movement is grounded in the idea that everyone, regardless of race, skin color, and national origin, is guaranteed equal rights and treatment before the law. As Martin Luther King pointed out in the 1963 March on Washington, the Declaration of Independence was a "promissory note to which every American was to fall heir. This note was the promise that all men, yes, black men as well as white men, would be guaranteed the unalienable rights of life, liberty, and the pursuit of happiness." Equality is a noble virtue for which we should all be committed to advancing. However, in the education setting, equity, not equality, should be our guiding principle. No other issue is as crucial to an effective 21st-century education as educational equity because only through equitable approaches can educators provide equal opportunities for all students to be successful.

Equality means treating every student the same regardless of circumstances. And while on the surface, equality may seem like a virtue, it is not when one considers that every student is an individual with unique needs and circumstances and that treating students equally is inherently unfair to those students who need support to achieve academic success. Some examples of equity may include approaches that welcome, value, and nurture culturally and socioeconomically diverse learners. For instance, equity means assisting English language learners and recent arrivals to the United States to help them adjust to their new setting. Educational equity means providing for students' physical needs of food, health, and hygiene so that they can focus on learning and not survival. Additionally, educating students equitably means caring for their social and emotional needs.

For example, childhood and adolescence can be challenging but may be worse for students who experience bullying because of their identities across the LGBTQIA+ spectrum. Equity means providing support and services for students who struggle to learn due to physical, mental, and intellectual challenges. Finally, equity means making the school a welcoming place for students' families so that they have agency in making decisions that impact their student's education. Much has been written about the necessity of school equity as it applies to children with physical and intellectual challenges, and rightfully so.

Objectives:

- Describe how the nation's changing demographics require a new approach to teaching diverse learners.

- Explain how culturally responsive teaching and curriculum can help historically marginalized students achieve academic success.

- Identify the principles of social and emotional learning, and how to apply them in your own setting.

5.1 Schools Changing Demographics and the Need for Change

The nation is changing quickly as the country's population continues to grow in size and diversity. In 2020, the United States topped 331 million people, becoming the third-most populous nation in the world after China and India. Ten years from now, demographers predict the U.S. population will swell to over 350 million. As the population grows, it is becoming more diverse. The U.S. Census Bureau projects that by 2050 the nation will become "minority white." Caucasians will comprise 49.7 percent, Latinx 24.6 percent, Blacks 13.1 percent, Asians 7.9 percent, and multiracial people 3.8 percent. A variety of factors have contributed to this demographic shift, but the most significant are immigration and the growth of minority groups. Combined racial minorities will grow by 74 percent, while the White population will see a natural decrease as its population grows older and has fewer children. According to the U.S. Census Bureau, the effects of the demographic shift can already be seen with younger citizens as Whites under the age of fifteen are already an ethnic minority in the United States.

Immigration continues to play a significant role in the nation's demographic change. As of 2017, 44 million foreign-born people live here, comprising 13.6 percent of the total population. Compare that to 1965, when immigrants were only 5 percent of the total population. Latinx people make up the largest block of ethnic minorities totaling over 59 million in 2017 or 17.8 percent. Latinx refers to a person of Latin American origin or descent and is used as a gender-neutral or nonbinary alternative to Latino or Latina. To illustrate how significant this demographic shift is, consider that in 1980 there were approximately 14.8 million Latinx people who made up only 6.5 percent of the population. However, Mexicans continue to make up the largest subpopulation of immigrants, as 28 percent of all immigrants were born in Mexico. In one of the most massive demographic shifts in modern immigration history, Mexican immigration has seen a significant reversal. Between 2009 and 2015, more Mexicans have left the United States than arrived. Additionally, undocumented immigration from Mexico has leveled off. While immigration from Mexico has decreased, immigration from Asia is growing. Demographers project Asians to become the largest immigration group by 2065, comprising 38 percent of all immigrants surpassing Latinx, making up 31 percent in the same period. Chinese, Filipinos, and Indians make up the largest Asian subgroups.

The changing demographics have profoundly affected American life, including the economy, politics, entertainment, and education. Public schools have witnessed dramatic changes as a result of the demographic shift. According to the 2010 U.S. census, primary and secondary schools' total enrollment reached 54.2 million and is expected to grow to 56.4 million students in 2020. Student populations reflect the nation's changing demographics and are becoming more linguistically and ethnically diverse than ever. According to James Woodworth, commissioner of the National Center for Education Statistics (NCES), "Between fall 2000 and fall 2017, the percentage of public-school students who were White decreased from 61 to 48 percent, and the percentage of students who were Black decreased from 17 to 15 percent. In contrast, the percentage of Hispanic public-school students increased from 16 to 27 percent during the same period."

Before I became a teacher, I sold washers and dryers at Sears located at the Boulevard Mall in Las Vegas, just a few miles off the strip. In the mid-1990s, before the Great Recession, people were buying new homes and appliances at a furious pace. It was a great part-time job because, on a good weekend, I could earn several hundred dollars in commission. The demographics in the surrounding neighborhood were changing quickly, and more of our customers were working-class Spanish speakers. Wanting to sell appliances to as many customers as possible, I began to teach myself Spanish. I started reading the Spanish translation of appliance manuals so that I could point out all of the features and benefits in the hopes of closing the sale. Additionally, I was lucky enough to have a colleague who taught me enough Spanish to muddle through a transaction. On slow nights I made Spanish flashcards and spent hours memorizing words and expressions. Despite the difficulties, learning Spanish has been an immensely satisfying endeavor both personally and professionally. As someone who has tried to learn a second language, I understand how difficult it is. I can empathize with students and their families who are going through the process because it isn't easy. Additionally, I like to use Spanish with my Spanish-speaking students. Even though they are all fluent in English, the looks on their faces when I speak a few words to them are priceless. Using Spanish demonstrates to my students that I value and appreciate the Spanish language and culture, and it deepens our relationship.

5.2   The Achievement Gap

Despite public education's mission to help each child realize their academic potential, there is a persistent achievement gap between White-Black and White-Latinx students. The achievement gap is a disparity in academic performance between groups of students. There are different ways that an achievement gap can manifest itself and this includes grades, standardized test scores, course selection, dropout rates, and college completion rates. The National Assessment for Educational Progress (NAEP), also referred to as the nation's report card, is an assessment administered by the Department of Education that measures what students know and can do in various subjects, including mathematics, reading, writing, science, and history. The NAEP test given in 2009 revealed that despite overall rising scores for Black and Hispanic students, they still trail their White and Asian peers by over 20 test-score points on fourth- and eighth-grade reading and math tests. This disparity is the equivalent of about two grade levels worth of learning.

Additionally, the distribution of the achievement gap is not even across the country. According to the Stanford Center for Educational Policy Analysis, the White-Black achievement gap is most pronounced in the upper Midwest in states like Wisconsin, Michigan, Illinois, and Minnesota. States with small populations of Black students see smaller achievement gaps, such as in West Virginia, Hawaii, Idaho, Wyoming, Montana, Vermont, and New Hampshire. The same is true for the White-Latinx achievement gap. The gap is most profound in the New England states and California, Colorado, Minnesota, and the District of Columbia. The report goes on to indicate that the achievement gaps have been narrowing since the 1990s. Many believe this is because Black and Latinx students' scores have improved faster than White students.

The ACT, the nation's most widely used college entrance exam, is another data point that illustrates the achievement gap. The 2017 test scores show that only 9 percent of students from low-income families whose parents did not go to college and identified as Black, Latinx, American Indian, or Pacific Islander were well prepared for college. Conversely, students not reflecting those characteristics were six times more prepared for higher education. Additionally, students of color are not graduating high school at the same rates as White students. According to the Annie E. Casey Foundation's 2020 Kids Count Data Book in the 2017–18 school year, 11 percent of Whites did not finish high school on time. The rate for high school non-completion for African Americans was 21 percent, Latinx was 19 percent, and American Indians was 27 percent.

The achievement gap is the result of a complex mixture of interrelated causes. These various factors "are actively and passively undermining widespread academic excellence among Black students attending urban schools. Race- and class-based inequalities create and perpetuate the unequal distribution of educational resources, which sustains the Black-White achievement gap" (Lewis, James, Hancock, & Hill-Jackson, 2008). According to the U.S. Census Bureau,

79 percent of fourth graders in low-income families are not proficient in reading compared with 50 percent in moderate- to high-income families. Unfortunately, the zip code in which a student lives is a significant predictor of future health, education, and success. A recent report from Georgetown University revealed that students with higher socioeconomic status (SES) have an educational safety net. Meaning, if they slip academically, they can recover much more readily than those with low SES. The ability to rebound from academic danger is because students from the middle and upper classes have access to tutors, credit retrieval, and various technologies that can make catching up easier. Further, students with higher SES are admitted to four-year universities at much higher rates (46%) than those at the bottom of the socioeconomic ladder (14%). A student's SES plays a significant role in high school test scores and college attainment. According to the report, the students with the highest SES with bottom-half math scores are more likely to complete college than the lowest SES students with top-half math scores. This is fundamentally antithetical to the American ethos that all people have an equal opportunity to succeed with hard work and determination.

TEACHING STRATEGY:

The achievement gap is the result of a wide variety of in-school and out-of-school factors. Since out-of-school factors are often "gravity problems," teachers should focus their energy on the things they can control in their classrooms and schools. One idea is to create wraparound services such as a classroom or school food pantry and clothes closet. Students will not learn effectively until their basic needs are met first. Providing students with snacks, school supplies, personal hygiene products, and clothing items can make a big difference in a students' life and their ability to learn.

Additionally, teachers could use the food pantry as a jumping-off point to provide students with information about other community resources and provide emotional support for students experiencing trauma. Teachers can secure resources for their pantries through grant writing, developing partnerships with local charities and food pantries, or other fundraising methods. Teachers could also solicit support from parents to volunteer in the distribution and organization of the pantry, which is an excellent way to build school-community partnerships.

In addition, the achievement gap has financial implications not only for the students who have fallen behind but also for the American economy. The Bureau of Labor Statistics reported that in 2019 an individual without a high school diploma had a median weekly income of only $606 compared to $749 for high school graduates. Workers with some college or an associate degree earned $875 a week, while those earning a college degree had average weekly earnings of $1,281. Those who earned advanced or professional degrees had weekly earnings of $1,559. The achievement gap negatively impacts individuals financially but has a tremendous drag on the American economy. According to the McKinsey & Company report that examined the impact of the achievement gap in America's schools, closing the achievement gap would result in greater worker productivity resulting in the growth of GDP. The report estimates that "if the United States had in recent years closed the gap between its educational achievement levels and those of better-performing nations such as Finland and Korea, GDP in 2008 could have been $1.3 trillion to $2.3 trillion higher. This represents 9 to 16 percent of GDP" (2009). In addition to billions of dollars lost to the American economy, one must also consider the squandered potential of gifted and talented students across the country who were left to languish in failing classrooms and schools. Instead of going to college and founding businesses, and innovating the next big ideas that could change the world, many victims of the achievement gap will experience overall lower earnings, poorer health, and higher rates of incarceration according to a report published by the NAACP (2011).

5.3 From Dependent to Independent Learners

The achievement gap between Blacks, Hispanics, and Asian and White students and students in poverty is not a matter based solely on ability. Rather, it is a lack of opportunity. The opportunity gap is due to many factors, including unequal access to skilled teachers, a high-quality curriculum, and large class sizes. The discrepancy in educational outcomes can be attributed to the

American school system's unequal opportunities, one of the most unequal in the industrialized world (Darling-Hammond, 2016). A general rule of thumb is that students from more affluent backgrounds receive a better public education than those from less affluent backgrounds (Garcia & Weiss, 2017). Unlike European and Asian nations that fund public education equally, local property taxes support local schools. In this country, the wealthiest 10 percent of American school districts spend on average ten times more on education than the poorest 10 percent (Darling-Hammond, 2016). Zip code and homeownership should not be a predictor of a child's educational opportunities, but unfortunately, that is the reality. One of the opportunity gap results is that students from "good" schools become independent learners, while those in "bad" schools become dependent learners. It should be every teacher, school, and district's goal to provide their students with the knowledge, skills, and dispositions to become lifelong learners to reduce the achievement gap and provide a high-quality education for all students.

In less advantaged schools, students generally receive fewer opportunities to develop essential skills to become independent learners. The lack of opportunity may be due to teachers who do not have high expectations for what their students can do and, as a result, rely on lectures, the textbook, and worksheets to drive their curriculum without regard for students' likes and differences. In his seminal article, "The Pedagogy of Poverty Versus Good Teaching," Martin Haberman (1991) outlines the characteristics of the 'pedagogy of poverty,' which permeates urban classrooms. In these schools, most of the learning activities revolve around the teacher, such as asking questions, giving directions, monitoring seatwork, giving tests, assigning homework, and grading. Teachers do most of the heavy intellectual lifting, and through direct instruction, tell students what they need to know. As a result, these students get trapped in a cycle of mind-numbing busy work with little intellectual or personal satisfaction attached. Because the student is so dependent on the teacher to direct learning experiences, students are unsure how to tackle unfamiliar tasks or problems. Unable to move forward without the teacher's assistance, students learn helplessness and frequently sit passively until they intercede and solve students' problems for them. The pedagogy of poverty teaches students compliance through punishment and reward mechanisms, in which quiet obedience is a virtue and the mark of a good teacher. Students reward teachers with on-task behaviors as long as they do not require them to do too much. As Haberman points out (1991), "The pedagogy of poverty requires that teachers who begin their careers intending to be helpers, models, guides, stimulators, and caring sources of encouragement transform themselves into the directive, authoritarians to function in urban schools." This symbiotic relationship results in passive students who are unable and unwilling to take responsibility for their learning.

It should be the goal of all learning institutions, urban and rural, rich and poor, to transform students into independent lifelong learners. Due to the rapid development of new technologies and access to unprecedented information levels, it is not enough that students graduate high school possessing static levels of basic knowledge. To be competitive in today's knowledge economy, students need to be independent learners who take responsibility for their learning. They need to ask the right questions, propose solutions based on sound research and reason, and communicate effectively verbally and in writing. Students need to work productively individually and as members of teams. They must be flexible and understand that the state of knowledge is fluid and adapt to changes quickly. Students need to be culturally conversant and develop understanding and empathy for culturally different people from being successful in a diverse workplace.

Further, independent learners must possess the grit to overcome setbacks. Professor of psychology and author Angela Duckworth describes grit as passion and perseverance for long-term goals over an extended time. Gritty students develop a "growth mindset" or the idea that learning is not fixed and can grow and change with effort. Students do not develop grit by completing worksheets, listening to lectures, or taking multiple-choice tests. Instead, they become independent, lifelong, gritty students by engaging in meaningful learning tasks with high cognitive demand. Teachers can help students develop grit by being warm demanders who have high expectations of all students. Failure is not an option, and teachers provide their students with opportunities to reflect and improve.

Teachers can help students become independent lifelong learners by providing them with rigorous learning activities that require a high degree of cognitive effort. Norman Webb's Depth of Knowledge (DOK) levels can help teachers calibrate their practice to achieve this goal. Students engage in recall and reproduction of information at the lowest levels of cognitive depth and engage in activities that require knowledge of some skills and concepts. Classrooms with primarily dependent learners generally work at these levels. Students learn to be independent learners at the highest DOK level by engaging in learning activities requiring them to think critically and analytically. They do this by engaging in the synthesis of multiple sources of information and interpret various representations. They transfer knowledge from one domain to another to solve problems and examine enduring controversies, usually over long periods of time. Further, independent learners identify significant concepts and central ideas as opposed to isolated facts. They have agency in their learning and have opportunities to demonstrate voice and choice, and are active participants in the learning activities that address real-world problems. Finally, independent learners question conventional wisdom, challenge the status quo, and engage in reflective practices to achieve self-improvement and intellectual growth.

One of the primary purposes of education is to transform dependent learners into independent learners. But this is easier said than done. Implementing new pedagogies and approaches is a perennial challenge in education because traditional points of view and the status quo are the path of least resistance. Most traditional schools do not support independent learners' development, and those intransigent teachers who try to buck the system are usually met with student resistance. After all, the sit and get approach is cognitively less demanding than the heavy intellectual lifting required of dependent learners. Culturally responsive pedagogy is a practical and research-based approach to raising the student achievement of all learners.

TEACHING STRATEGY:

An effective strategy to develop students' critical thinking skills and independent learning is to teach them how to ask their own questions. Developed by the Right Question Institute, the Question Formulation Technique, or QFT, helps students create their own questions to build learning skills, self-advocacy, and democratic action. The QFT can be used with students of all ages and developmental levels and subjects. To learn more about this approach, visit the Right Question Institute website or the Harvard Graduate School of Education online workshop called Teaching Students to Ask Their Own Questions: Best Practices in the Question Formulation Technique.

5.4 Culturally Responsive Teaching

Culturally relevant teaching honors the students' sense of humanity and dignity. Their complete personhood is never doubted. Self-worth and self-concept is promoted in a very basic way, by acknowledging the individual's worthiness to be part of a supportive and loving group.

—GLORIA LADSON-BILLINGS

The teaching force in our public schools has remained static over the years, despite the nation's rapidly changing demographics. According to the National Center for Education Statistics, educators are overwhelmingly female, White, middle-class, and middle-aged. Women comprise 76 percent of all educators in the nation's K-12 public schools. In elementary school, that number jumps to 89 percent. Further, 79 percent of teachers reported that they are White, typically earn around $63,645 a year, and average forty-three years of age (Digest of Education Statistics, 2020). On the other hand, Latinx teachers represent only about 9 percent of the teaching force, Blacks 7 percent, and Asians 2 percent (Taie & Westat, 2020). The Brookings Institute recently reported that just 20 percent of the public-school workforce reported that they identify as people of color, while over 50 percent of the study body does. That is a representation gap of 30 percent. Further, researchers point out that a more diverse workforce provides long-lasting benefits to students of color (Hansen & Quintero, 2021). The number of teachers from diverse backgrounds has been growing since the late 1980s but still has a long way to go before they proportionally represent the students of color they teach. As a result, the teachers leading most classrooms represent the mores, values, and points of view of the dominant culture and may have difficulty working with students from cultures different than their own. And while many teachers work tirelessly to deliver the best possible education to all of their students, without regard to their race, socioeconomic, and language status, cultural misunderstandings may cause some teachers to view their students of color through a deficit lens (Douglas, Lewis, Douglas, Scott, & Garrison-Wade, 2008).

According to professor of urban education Richard Milner, deficit thinking is "teachers' perceptions that students of color do not already possess the necessary skills, knowledge, and attitudes to succeed and learn, and can result in the development of curriculum and instruction that falls short of optimal teaching and learning" (Milner, 2006, p. 80). In other words, some educators view students of color and their communities as "problems" that need to be fixed, rather than as allies and partners in their education. As professors of education Lori Patton and Samuel Museus (2019) point out, "Deficit thinking is rooted in a blame the victim orientation that suggests that people are responsible for their predicament and fails to acknowledge that they live within coercive systems that cause harm with no accountability." Part of the educational "system" that has contributed to deficit thinking is the inability or lack of interest by some educators to build cultural bridges to their students, which could be an essential factor in their students' academic success (Douglas et al., 2008). In her seminal book *Other People's Children: Cultural Conflict in the Classroom*, Lisa Delpit (2006) argues that there are two areas in which White teachers and their students of color experience cultural misunderstandings. The first is the teacher's misunderstanding of their students' "aptitudes, intent, or abilities," where the misinterpretation may result from differences in language use and interactional patterns. The second area of cultural misunderstanding stems from pedagogies that are incongruent with historically marginalized students. Delpit points out that "teachers may utilize styles of instruction and discipline that are at odds with community norms," resulting in a cultural incongruence between students and teachers (p. 167).

According to Lisa Delpit, schools, classrooms, curriculum, and resources such as textbooks generally reflect the power, norms, and expectations of the middle class that produced them. There are codes and rules for participating in power, which she calls the "culture of power." Embedded throughout the "culture of power" are the unspoken but established rules of the dominant culture necessary to succeed in school and career, such as speaking, writing, dressing, and interacting with others. Delpit points out that those who have the power are least likely to acknowledge its existence. At the same time, those that don't are coerced into conforming to it. I am guilty of making this mistake. Like many teachers, I associated African American Vernacular English (AAVE) with slang. I didn't understand that AAVE is a dialect of SAE that consists of complex grammar, vocabulary, rhetorical patterns, semantics, and pronunciation. To help my students speak properly, I would "correct" them when they used improper verb tenses, double negatives, and so on. I now approach AAVE much differently. I use AAVE as an opportunity to discuss with students how language and power are related. Judith Butler, president of the Modern Language Association, points out the importance of students being trilingual. Trilingualism suggests that there are three variations of the English language, the home dialect, the formal dialect, and the professional dialect. According to Butler, each form of English is legitimate and proper, but context dictates which form of English is appropriate. Using Butler's framework, I can acknowledge and celebrate students' home dialects, and at the same time, help students become successful in navigating formal and professional dialects.

As a result of school desegregation in the 1960s and 1970s, educators have tried to teach students of color through various multicultural education approaches such as culturally appropriate, culturally congruent, culturally responsive, and culturally compatible teaching (Aronson & Laughter, 2016). These frameworks suggest that to raise student achievement for historically marginalized students, schools should reflect students' diverse cultures by infusing the curriculum with the histories, contributions, and achievements of diverse actors. Building on the framework of multicultural education, two dominant strands emerged distinct from earlier methodologies. In the mid-1970s, Geneva Gay outlined the principles of culturally responsive teaching, which focused on the teaching process or what teachers do in the classroom. In contrast, Gloria Ladson-Billings developed culturally relevant pedagogy as a theoretical framework to examine multiple aspects of student achievement.

Geneva Gay described culturally responsive teaching "as using the cultural knowledge, prior experience, frames of reference, and performance styles of ethnically diverse students to make learning encounters more relevant to and effective for them" (Gay, 2010, p. 36). Gay focused her research on what teachers do in the classroom, and according to her, eight dimensions characterize culturally responsive teaching:

⊃ Validation

Culturally responsive teaching validates students' culture and believes that it is worthy of being taught in the formal curriculum by infusing cultural information, resources, and materials in all content and skills taught in school. Additionally, teachers validate students' lived experiences and build bridges to the school by utilizing a wide range of educational approaches that capitalize on students' interests and learning styles.

⊃ Comprehensive and Inclusive

Culturally responsive teachers help students of color achieve academically and maintain students' cultural identity and connections to their community by developing camaraderie and shared responsibility. In other words, teachers help students build a community of learners in which all students are expected to learn and achieve at high levels.

⊃ Multidimensional

Culturally responsive teachers utilize various, overlapping factors like curriculum content that reflects the diversity of learners. Teachers understand the racial, sociopolitical teaching context to build a classroom climate that elevates academic achievement for all learners. Teachers utilize various instructional tools and approaches that build on diverse students' strengths and help them improve upon their weaknesses.

⊃ Empowering

Culturally responsive teachers empower their students to be successful by imbuing within them confidence, courage, and the belief that they can achieve their goals. These teachers encourage students to take intellectual risks and persevere in the face of challenges and adversity.

⊃ Transformative

Culturally responsive teachers engage in the work of transformation by first identifying the strengths and accomplishments of diverse students, then enhancing these strengths through the instructional process. Students' academic success and cultural consciousness take place in tandem as students build cultural pride and awareness.

⊃ **Emancipatory**

> Culturally responsive teaching is psychologically and intellectually liberating for students of color because they are exposed to knowledge beyond the mainstream canon.

⊃ **Humanistic**

> Culturally responsive teachers uphold all students' welfare, dignity, and respect across ethnic, racial, and social groups.

⊃ **Ethical**

> Culturally responsive teachers are ethical in that they dismantle the hegemony of the dominant culture on educational policies and practices. They interrupt the notion that education is "cultureless" and unbiased.

Gloria Ladson-Billings introduced the idea of culturally relevant pedagogy, which she describes as "a pedagogy that empowers students intellectually, socially, emotionally, and politically by using cultural referents to impart knowledge, skills, and attitudes" (Ladson-Billings, 1994, p. 17–18). She designed the framework after observing successful teachers of African American students and noting their beliefs and ideologies toward educating students of color. The framework consists of three main components. The first and most important aspect of culturally relevant pedagogy focuses on student learning and academic achievement. Successful teachers of historically marginalized students have high expectations for all students and believe that all students can succeed academically. In other words, teachers see all of their students as being uniquely brilliant. In addition, teachers must possess knowledge and skills in developing students' cultural competence. This means that students must be able to maintain their cultural integrity while being academically successful. Successful teachers achieve this aim by helping students navigate between their home culture and school culture by acknowledging and pushing back against the implicit bias built into the institution. Lastly, culturally responsive pedagogy means that teachers help their students engage in learning tasks that require them to "recognize, understand and critique current social inequities" (Ladson-Billings, 1995, p. 476). Critical consciousness must begin with the teacher, who must recognize sociopolitical issues of race, class, and gender within themselves before integrating them into the curriculum (Aronson & Laughter, 2016).

Despite their subtle differences, Gay and Ladson-Billings's frameworks share four commonalities in elevating student achievement for diverse students (Aronson & Laughter 2016). The first criterion is that culturally relevant educators use constructivist approaches to help students build bridges between their life experience and new academic knowledge. In other words, they use students' knowledge and cultural assets as a vehicle to raise academic achievement. In addition, culturally relevant teachers engage their students in critical reflection by examining issues pertaining to their own lives and society. Teachers accomplish this aim by introducing students to a culturally relevant curriculum that includes diverse viewpoints and challenges conventional norms. Further, culturally relevant teachers facilitate students' cultural competence so that they learn to value, appreciate, and take pride in their own culture and other cultures. Cultural awareness is a valuable 21st-century skill in an increasingly global economy. Finally, culturally relevant teachers help their students identify and challenge historic power differentials through critical pedagogy. Paulo Friere (2018) describes critical pedagogy as "learning to perceive social, political, and economic contradictions, and to take action against oppressive elements of reality" (p. 35).

Not only is culturally relevant teaching effective in building students' sense of belonging, inclusion, and cultural pride, but it is an effective way to increase academic outcomes for all learners. The research concludes that culturally responsive teaching has an overall positive effect on student learning across multiple content areas such as math, science, and English for historically marginalized students and students of the dominant culture (Aronson & Laughter, 2016). For example, culturally relevant approaches can increase students' motivation and interest in the subjects they are studying, leading to an increased ability to engage in content area discourse and investigations. Increased student engagement is directly correlated to higher student achievement. Further, culturally relevant teaching can increase student perceptions of themselves as capable students. When students believe they can be academically successful, they usually are.

TEACHING STRATEGY:

Culturally responsive inquiry learning or CRIL. CRIL is a teaching and learning approach at the nexus of inquiry-based learning and culturally responsive pedagogy. I designed the approach to create independent thinkers through learning activities that require high cognitive demand while teaching students 21st-century learning skills such as critical thinking, creativity, collaboration, and communication. Additionally, CRIL utilizes aspects of critical pedagogy to provide students an opportunity to investigate the causes and legacies of social, political, and economic inequities. Finally, I designed CRIL to increase student academic achievement, particularly for historically marginalized students, by linking inquiry to social justice and equity issues. These skills will enable students to meet the challenges of the knowledge economy while at the same time help them understand the roots of societal inequities in the pursuit of change. Please see my lesson Hip Hop Herstory: African American Women Computers for an example of CRIL.

5.5 The Culturally Responsive Curriculum

According to the U.S. Department of Education, the high school dropout rate had decreased from 8.3 percent in 2010 to 5.1 percent in 2019. Despite the good news, there is still cause for concern because, unfortunately, students of color drop out of school at higher rates than their White peers. For example, according to the U.S. Department of Education, National Center for Education Statistics, in 2019, Latinx students dropped out at a rate of 7.7 percent, and Black students 5.6 percent. In comparison, White students dropped out of school at a rate of 4.1 percent, and Asian students dropped out at only 1.9 percent. The disparity in dropout rates is complex and multifaceted and indicates the persistent achievement gap in our public schools. There are two main categories for why students of color may leave school without a degree. Out-of-school causes may include the challenges of living in poverty, drug/alcohol abuse, chronic absenteeism, pregnancy, learning disabilities, domestic and community violence, various forms of abuse and neglect, and the fact that many students need to work to support themselves and their families. In-school causes may include unnecessarily harsh disciplinary action such as out-of-school suspensions for minor infractions of school rules, low expectations, lack of meaningful adult relationships at school, erroneous special education placement, poor academic achievement, and boredom resulting from a curriculum lacking relevance and connection to students' lives. A Harvard University article, "Bored Out of their Minds," points out that over half of all dropouts cite boredom for their decision to leave school (Jason, 2017). For students of color, a Eurocentric curriculum dominated by the experiences and points of view of the dominant culture may lead to indifference and disengagement from historically marginalized students who may find difficulty relating and connecting to the curriculum. The research bears this out too. Researchers from Stanford University examined data from a pilot program in San Francisco in which high school students considered to be at an elevated risk of dropping out were enrolled in an ethnic studies course. The results were staggering. Attendance rose by 21 percent, grade-point averages rose by 1.4 percent, and students enrolled in the ethnic studies course earned on average twenty-three more credits toward graduation than did similar at-risk students who did not take the course (Washington, 2018).

Culturally responsive teachers help relate the curriculum to students' lives by using a culturally responsive curriculum or CRC. The curriculum is broadly defined as the "totality of student experiences that occur in the educational process" and consists of educational standards and goals, content, learning experiences, and evaluation of student learning (Kelly, 2009). A CRC goes a step further by acknowledging that curriculum documents are not ideologically neutral. Instead, cultural artifacts must be critically analyzed to ensure equity in representation and freedom from implicit bias. They must also be aware of what is not covered in the curriculum in what is known as the excluded or null curriculum. In addition, culturally responsive teachers should be deliberate in selecting teaching materials to reflect the ethnic and linguistic diversity in the classroom to raise student engagement and achievement. As professor of education Geneva Gay points out, "The fundamental aim of culturally responsive pedagogy is to empower ethnically diverse students through academic success, cultural affiliation, and personal efficacy. Knowledge in the form of curriculum content is central to this empowerment" (Gay, 2019, p. 142).

TEACHING STRATEGY:

According to Geneva Gay (2002), the symbolic curriculum includes various cultural artifacts such as images, symbols, icons, mottoes, awards, and celebrations to impart knowledge, skills, morals, and values of diverse cultures to students. In classrooms and schools, the most common way to transmit the symbolic curriculum is through bulletin boards, posters, wall hangings, and murals. As a result, teachers should think deeply about what they are communicating to students with their symbolic curriculum. Since wall space is limited in schools, it is essential to think about what is displayed in school and what is not. Teachers should make an effort to reflect in the symbolic curriculum by displaying artifacts from a diversity of cultures, ages, genders, geographic locations, and social classes.

Teachers who employ a CRC help substantiate and legitimize their students' cultural backgrounds, including their histories, contributions, experiences, and perspectives into the curriculum. In the formal curriculum, White students have an easier time making meaning of their learning because they see themselves more often reflected in the curriculum materials that substantiate the dominant culture's narrative. Including the voices of diverse actors is vital because curriculum materials that reflect the students' culture may positively impact diverse learners' academic achievement by reducing feelings of alienation as they see themselves reflected in the subjects being studied (Stowe, 2017).

TEACHING STRATEGY:

Gloria Ladson-Billings suggests three things that teachers can do to create a CRC. The first is to deconstruct the curriculum. This means that teachers should take apart "official knowledge" to expose the weakness, omissions, distortions, and myths built into the curriculum. This will often require that teachers do their research and outside reading independent of the textbook, which serves as the basis for most programs of study. For example, a history teacher could read Howard Zinn's *A People's History of the United States,* Ibram X Kendi's *Stamped from the Beginning: The Definitive History of Racist Ideas in America,* and James Loewen's *Lies my Teacher Told Me: Everything Your American History Textbook Got Wrong.* Further, there are a host of online resources teachers can explore to expand their knowledge of diverse cultures and experiences. One of my favorite podcasts, for example, is *Teaching Hard History* produced by the Southern Poverty Law Center. There are also scores of massive open online courses or MOOCs. One of my favorites that features courses on just about every conceivable topic is Coursera.

The next step is to construct a culturally responsive curriculum based on the experiences and knowledge that students bring with them to the classroom. To do this effectively, teachers will have to make a great effort to get to know their students as individuals and learn about their individual experiences as it applies to the content. The final step is to reconstruct the curriculum to include filling the holes revealed through critical analysis of the curriculum. Teachers must be ready to help students challenge orthodoxy and established power structures as they question the content. Additionally, educators must approach their curriculum with intentionality. They must plan and implement culturally diverse actors, points of view, and experiences throughout their curriculum. Without deliberate planning and action, implementing a culturally responsive curriculum is just wishful thinking.

There are some stakeholders, however, who would argue that this critical approach to the curriculum is a form of indoctrination whose goal is to teach students to hate America. Or an attempt to make White students feel guilty for the atrocities committed in the nation's past. I respectfully disagree with this assertion. As a former marine who holds a master's degree in American history, I understand that teaching history is an academic pursuit governed by the established methodologies of the field. As a tweet from Librarianshipwreck points out, "Studying history will sometimes make you uncomfortable. Studying history will sometimes make you feel deeply upset. Studying history will sometimes make you feel extremely angry. If studying history always makes you feel proud and happy, you probably aren't studying history" (@libshipwreck, September 17, 2020). In science, for example, teachers teach evolutionary biology because it is an explanation of how organisms adapt to their environment and change over time based on the scientific evidence and supported by the Next Generation Science Standards. Science teachers are not labeled anti-American because they teach according to scientific principles that might make some people uncomfortable. Nor should it be anti-American to teach history that reveals the truth about America's past.

Finally, it should be noted that all academic disciplines will benefit from a CRC, not just the liberal arts subjects like history, literature, art history, philosophy, and foreign language and culture. Unfortunately, many teachers in STEM fields—science, technology, engineering, and mathematics—erroneously believe that because their discipline is "fact-based," the necessity for a culturally relevant curriculum is unnecessary. But research indicates the contrary is true. White men generally feel the greatest sense of belonging in STEM preparation programs, while women of color feel the least sense of belonging. According to Inside Higher Ed, there are many reasons for this to include the constant need for students of color to "prove" that they are academically worthy of being in the program, as well as feelings of exclusion from their institutions. Additionally, students of color experience a lack of representation that could lead to feelings of isolation and alienation that push them out of STEM majors at much higher rates than their White counterparts (Johnson & Elliott, 2020). In a moment when American educators are trying to lure more talented students into the STEM fields so that we can continue to be competitive in the global economy, we should be attracting more talented students into STEM fields and graduating them, not pushing them out.

5.6   Social-Emotional Learning (SEL)

The COVID-19 pandemic and quarantine during the 2020–2021 school year resulted in a year and a half of distance learning for most students in the public school system. Teachers and students had to learn quickly how to negotiate the digital technologies required to conduct school in a virtual environment. And while there was a steep learning curve for many, most would agree that utilizing these technologies overall was good. After all, virtual teaching and learning increased students' and teachers' proficiencies in using learning management systems and Google Workspace for Education Fundamentals such as Google Docs, Slides, Sheets, Drive, Forms, and Jamboard. Many teachers will continue to use these technologies as they return to in-person teaching, which will hopefully contribute to transforming "traditional" classroom spaces into hybrid learning environments. Despite these advancements, however, there have been significant challenges to learning online. As a result of the quarantine, students spent hours in front of a computer screen with few opportunities for social interaction and physical exercise, which according to the Center for Disease Control and Prevention, negatively impacted their emotional and mental well-being. This trauma was caused by abrupt changes to their routines, breaks in the continuity of their learning, disrupted health care, missed significant life events, and lost security and safety. In addition, students suffered from virtual learning fatigue, resulting from a lack of seeing other students' facial expressions, eye contact, and body language. Further, students had to contend with other stress-inducing factors such as family members' loss of employment, health emergencies, and various forms of abuse and neglect associated with the added stress of being in isolation, and in some cases, the death of a loved one. In other words, quarantine and distance learning has refocused the need for educators to practice social and emotional learning (SEL).

According to the Collaborative for Academic, Social, and Emotional Learning (CASEL), the goal of an SEL program is to foster the development of five interrelated sets of cognitive, affective, and behavioral competencies. These competencies can be taught to students of all ages from early childhood to adulthood in any subject area. SEL can be folded into already existing lessons with only slight modifications. In one of the most well-known large-scale studies of SEL, researcher Joseph Durlak and his associates conducted a meta-analysis of 213 school-based SEL programs in grades K–12 involving over 270,000 students. Research indicates that social-emotional learning increases social and emotional skills, boosts positive behavior, and improves academic achievement while lowering emotional distress levels and decreasing student conduct and behavioral problems (Durlak, Weissberg, Dymnicki, Taylor, & Schellinger, 2011). Research also indicates that SEL education has long-term benefits. In a 2012 meta-analysis of seventy-five previous studies, SEL and behavior programs have been shown to improve students' social, emotional well-being and attitudes up to seven months after receiving SEL instruction (Sklad, Diekstra, De Ritter, Ben, & Gravesteijn, 2012). Looking beyond formal SEL programs, a recent study of over 570,000 students demonstrated that individual teachers who introduce SEL approaches in their classrooms see an increase in positive student outcomes and behaviors and decreases in negative ones such as absences, suspensions, and dropouts (Jackson, 2018).

Early on during quarantine, I noticed that my students were beginning to disengage from their studies. Wanting to bring them a little joy, I started telling my students a joke of the day at the beginning of class. Because most of my students had their cameras off, it was difficult to tell their reactions to the jokes except for the occasional laughing emoji, or ha ha in the comments section. I had never told my students jokes before and honestly, felt corny doing it. One day I was pressed for time and did not prepare a joke. I thought my students wouldn't miss it. After all, they probably thought the jokes were stupid anyway. Boy, was I wrong. My students almost instantly began bombarding me with refrains of "Aren't you going to tell us a joke today?" So insistent they had become that I had no choice but to do a quick Google search and find them a few new jokes. At the end of the semester, I have my students complete a teacher evaluation, and the number one thing my students enjoyed about my class was the jokes! Many told me that the jokes brightened their day, giving them something to look forward to. What I've learned is that students appreciate the small things we do, even if they don't immediately show it. Every effort to make the class more interesting and enjoyable goes a long way to building positive relationships, especially if it requires you to move outside of your comfort zone.

▌ SELF-AWARE

Self-aware students know who they are. They have forged an identity by understanding their strengths and weaknesses and areas of academic and personal interest. They have a sense of confidence and purpose because they know their emotions, thoughts, and values and can utilize them to achieve their goals. They have a growth mindset and experience a high degree of self-efficacy due to positive self-images and perceptions. Self-aware students display honesty and integrity and actively monitor their biases and prejudices, which is essential for workers who will find themselves in increasingly diverse workspaces in the interconnected and global economy.

▌ SELF-MANAGEMENT

Self-management means that students can regulate their emotions, thoughts, and behaviors and delay gratification to pursue short-, medium-, and long-term goals. They have developed techniques that help them manage stress and understand the importance of emotional and physical self-care. In addition, good self-managers take the initiative and assume leadership roles when necessary to fulfill personal and collective objectives.

▌ SOCIAL AWARENESS

Socially aware students try to understand the perspectives of all people and continuously strive to empathize with people different from themselves (see more about social awareness in chapter 1). They seek to identify and dismantle institutional racism and are actively engaged in antiracist thinking. Those students who benefit from their privilege regarding race, gender, and socioeconomic backgrounds use their power to ally themselves with diverse actors in the fight for social and economic justice—understanding that their role is to support, not supplant, marginalized voices in the pursuit of equity.

RELATIONSHIP SKILLS

The ability to form healthy and supporting relationships with people of diverse backgrounds may be one of the most critical skills that students will need to succeed in the 21st-century economy. As workspaces become more diverse, students will need to communicate and collaborate across diverse cultures effectively. In addition, they must be skilled in constructive conflict resolution by having a high degree of cultural competency and empathy to avoid cultural misunderstandings.

RESPONSIBLE DECISION-MAKING

Life is about choices, and students need to make good decisions based on sound judgment and ethical standards. They need to analyze problems, including all available data and information, entertain a wide variety of solutions from various points of view, and understand how their decisions will affect others. Additionally, they must take responsibility and ownership of their choices and reflect on the consequences of their actions.

While social and emotional learning is a nonacademic subject, schools need to teach these skills to prepare their students to work effectively in the modern knowledge economy. In a recent *Forbes* magazine article, Byron Sanders points out, "An emerging benefit of explicit SEL instruction is that it builds the emotional intelligence and agility that business and industry is starting to name among the most desired workforce skills. For both their well-being and their future economic opportunities, SEL is power" (Sanders, 2020). In other words, if students are to be successful in the 21st-century economy, it is vital that they possess the skills and dispositions that will help them become more effective at regulating their emotions, better communicators, collaborators, and conflict resolvers. In addition, workers in the 21st century will need to possess the cultural competency to negotiate the challenges of working cross-culturally in an increasingly shrinking world.

TEACHING STRATEGY:

Many teachers may be thinking great, "one more thing" to do in an already dense curriculum with too little time. How in the world am I going to be able to implement social-emotional learning? The answer is that with a little intentionality and forethought, you can seamlessly add social and emotional learning into your daily lessons. An effective way to do this is by verbalizing what social-emotional core competency you want students to incorporate. Display a poster in your classroom that outlines the five core competencies for easy reference. Teachers can help students become more **self-aware** by having students pair up at the beginning of class and do a "check-in" so that you can gauge their emotional well-being and the "temperature of the room." Tell students, "Before we begin today's lesson, I want to get a sense of where we are emotionally." Pear Deck has some tremendous free starter screens for you to use with your students. You can help your students practice **self-management** by explicitly asking them, "What have you done today or are planning to do that will help you achieve your short-, medium-, and long-range goals?" You could do this as part of a warm-up activity or as an exit ticket. Help your students practice social awareness by intentionally examining various points of view of a topic under study. For example, in a history class studying the Great Depression, the teacher could ask, "How did the Great Depression impact people of color, the poor, or women?" Many teachers are already helping students build their **relationship skills** when they engage their students in collaborative learning strategies such as think-pair-share, the jigsaw method, or other team-building exercises. Be intentional, tell students, "For this exercise, I want you to concentrate on your communication skills, express yourself succinctly and clearly, make sure that your audience understands the point of your message." Teach students **responsible decision-making** by providing them with the seven-step decision-making model. You could practice by having students think about what college they want to go to. Say to students, "Today, you are going to decide on what college you want to attend based on the following decision-making steps."

The seven-step decision-making model

Step 1	Identify the problem
Step 2	Gather relevant information
Step 3	Identify the alternatives
Step 4	Weigh the evidence
Step 5	Choose the best solution among other options
Step 6	Take action
Step 7	Review the decision and its consequences (good & bad).

5.8   Questions for Reflection

1. What are some approaches and techniques educators can employ to effectively teach diverse learners?

2. What is culturally responsive teaching? What are some examples of culturally responsive pedagogy, and why is it beneficial for all students?

3. Why is social-emotional learning important for students to be successful in the 21st-century knowledge economy?

4. Why is it important that educators transform dependent learners into independent learners? What are some concrete things educators can do?

5. What are some practical strategies teachers can take to become social and emotional educators?

Conclusion

It is impossible to know what the future will bring, but if the past is prologue, it most assuredly it will look very different than the world does today. To be successful in whatever the future holds, students will need an education for the 21st Century to equip them with the knowledge, skills, and dispositions to help them be successful in an increasingly shrinking, technologically rich and culturally diverse world. Preparing students for the future will not be easy. It will require educators to have deep knowledge of the art and science of teaching and learning to include the implementation of student-centered, real-world learning that provides students opportunities to develop 21st century skills. Teachers must know how to create positive classroom and school cultures by having high expectations for all learners and by tapping into student's families, communities, and cultures to drive student achievement. Finally, to educate students for a rapidly changing and diversifying world, teachers must utilize culturally responsive pedagogy, and social and emotional learning techniques to help students navigate the complexities of the modern world.

It is my sincere hope that educators, and stakeholders of all types in the education space find some value in this book. I wrote it to share with others what I believe to be integral components of a 21st century education. It is based on over 20 years of classroom teaching the latest research, and a lot of reflection, and covers the minimum of what I think professional educators should know and be able to do in the modern classroom. However, I would like to acknowledge that this book is not the last word on effective teaching, educators may disagree with what I have included or omitted, and all mistakes are mine alone. Thank you for reading, and I wish you the best of luck as you prepare your students for the future by providing them an education for the 21st century.

References

2020 Kids Count Data Book (Rep.). (2022, June 22). Retrieved September/ October 2020, from https://www.aecf.org/resources/2020-kids-count-data-book/?gclid=CjwKCAjw8MD7BRArEiwAGZsrBSAya4nOHKBW 4T3_ZHKpPfzz9R7jOA4oU-smCjyChODZf3C5tcx2JhoCixcQAvD_ BwE#Education

Abrami, P. C., Bernard, R. M., Borokhovski, E., Waddington, D. I., Wade, C. A., & Persson, T. (2015). Strategies for teaching students to think critically: A meta-analysis. *Review of Educational Research, 85(2), 275-314.*

Achievement Gaps. (n.d.). Retrieved September 26, 2020, from https://nces. ed.gov/nationsreportcard/studies/gaps/

Achievement Gaps: How Hispanic and White Students in Public Schools Perform in Mathematics and Reading on the National Assessment of Educational Progress (Rep.). (2011, June 23). Retrieved September 25, 2020, from U.S. Department of Education website: https://nces.ed.gov/ nationsreportcard/pdf/studies/2011485.pdf

Adamson, F., & Darling-Hammond, L. (2012) Funding disparities and the inequitable distribution of teachers: Evaluating sources and solutions. Education Policy Analysis Archives, 20(37).

Agarwal, P. K., Nunes, L. D., & Blunt, J. R. (2021). Retrieval Practice Consistently Benefits Student Learning: a Systematic Review of Applied Research in Schools and Classrooms. Educational Psychology Review. https://doi. org/10.1007/s10648-021-09595-9

Alexander, R.J. (2012). Moral panic, miracle cures and educational policy: What can we really learn from international comparisons? *Scottish Educational Review, 4-21*

Allen, J., Gregory, A., Mikami, A., Lun, J., Hamre, B., & Pianta, R. (2013). Observations of effective teacher-student interactions in secondary school classrooms: predicting student achievement with the classroom assessment scoring system-secondary. *School psychology review, 42*(1), 76–98.

Alsalhi, N. R., Eltahir, M. E., & Al-Qatawneh, S. S. (2019). The effect of blended learning on the achievement of ninth grade students in science and their attitudes towards its use. Heliyon, 5(9), e02424.

Ambrose, S., Bridges, M., & Lovett, M. (2010). *How learning works: 7 research-based principles for smart teaching.* San Francisco: John Wiley and Sons

Ansell, S. (2011, July 7). Achievement Gap. *Education Week.* Retrieved Month Day, Year from http://www.edweek.org/ew/issues/achievement-gap/

Araujo, L., Saltelli, A., & Schnepf, S. V. (2017). Do P.I.S.A. data justify PISA-based education policy? *International Journal of Comparative Education and Development, 19*(1), 20-34. doi:10.1108/ijced-12-2016-0023

Aronson, Brittany, & Laughter, Judson. (2016). The theory and practice of culturally relevant education: A synthesis of research across content areas. *Review of Educational Research, 86*(1), 163–206. https://doi.org/10.3102/0034654315582066

Barbe, Walter Burke; Swassing, Raymond H.; Milone, Michael N. (1979). Teaching through *modality strengths: concepts practices.* Columbus, Ohio: Zaner-Blose

Baron, K. (2017, January 27). Finding a Balance for the Federal Role in Education Policy. Retrieved November 30, 2020, from https://www.carnegiefoundation.org/blog/finding-a-balance-for-the-federal-role-in-education-policy/

Barshay, J. (2020). What 2018 P.I.S.A. international rankings tell us about U.S. schools. Retrieved November 23, 2020, from https://hechingerreport. org/what-2018-pisa-international-rankings-tell-us-about-u-s-schools/

Baumert, Jürgen & Kunter, Mareike. (2013). The Effect of Content Knowledge and Pedagogical Content Knowledge on Instructional Quality and Student Achievement. 10.1007/978-1-4614-5149-5_9.

Benabou, R., & Tirole, J. (2003). Intrinsic and Extrinsic Motivation. *Review of Economic Studies, 70(3)*, 489-520. doi:10.1111/1467-937x.00253

Ben-Peretz, M. (2011). Teacher knowledge: What is it? How do we uncover it? What are its implications for schooling? Teaching and Teacher Education, 27(1), 3-9. doi:10.1016/j.tate.2010.07.015

Benner, M., Jeffrey, A., & Brown, C. (2019, July). Elevating student voice in education. Retrieved February 27, 2021, from https://www. americanprogress.org/issues/education-

Black, P., & Wiliam, D. (1998). Assessment and classroom learning. Assessment in Education, 5(1), 7-75

Born to Win, Schooled to Lose: Why Equally Talented Students Don't Get Equal Chances to Be All They Can Be. CEW Georgetown. (2020, August 18). https://cew.georgetown.edu/cew-reports/schooled2lose/.

Bowen, R. S. (2017). Understanding by Design. Vanderbilt University Center for Teaching. Retrieved from https://cft.vanderbilt.edu/understanding-by-design/.k-12/reports/2019/08/14/473197/elevating-student-voice-education/

Brandt, W. C. (2020). Measuring student success skills: A review of the literature on self-direction. Dover, NH: National Center for the Improvement of Educational Assessment.

Bronte-Tinkew, J., & Redd, Z. (2001). Logic models and outcomes for youth entrepreneurship programs. DC Children and Youth Investment Corporation. http://www.childtrends.org/wp-content/ uploads/01/ Youth-Entrepreneurship-FINAL-Report.doc.

Brooks, J. G., & Brooks, M. G. (1999). In search of understanding: The case for constructivist classrooms. Alexandria, VA: Association for Supervision and Curriculum Development.

Bulger, S. M., Mohr, D. J., & Walls, R. T. (2002). Stack the deck in favor of your students by using the four aces of effective teaching. Journal of Effective Teaching, 5(2).

Bureau of Labor Statistics, U.S. Department of Labor, The Economics Daily, Median weekly earnings $606 for high school dropouts, $1,559 for advanced degree holders at https://www.bls.gov/opub/ted/2019/ median-weekly-earnings-606-for-high-school-dropouts-1559-for-advanced-degree-holders.htm (visited *June 14, 2021*).

Chen, Q. (2019, December 04). Nope, China isn't celebrating its big win in test scores. Here's why. Retrieved November 28, 2020, from https://www. inkstonenews.com/education/why-china-shrugs-its-return-top-spot-pisa-test/article/3040624

Cheryan, S., Ziegler, S. A., Plaut, V. C., & Meltzoff, A. N. (2014). Designing classrooms to maximize student achievement. *Policy Insights from the Behavioral and Brain Sciences, 1(1), 4–12.*

Chetty, R., Friedman, J., & Rockoff, J. (2013, September 12). Measuring the Impacts of Teachers II: Teacher Value-Added and Student Outcomes in Adulthood. Retrieved January 14, 2021, from https://www.nber.org/ papers/w19424

Chingos, M. (2016, July 29). Testing Costs a Drop in the Bucket. Retrieved December 03, 2020, from https://www.brookings.edu/blog/up-front/2015/02/02/testing-costs-a-drop-in-the-bucket/

Commarmond, I. (2017). In pursuit of a better understanding of and measure for entrepreneurial mindset. Retrieved from Cape Town, South Africa.

Condition of College and Career Readiness 2017 (Rep.). (2017, September 8). Retrieved September 27, 2020, from http://www.act.org/content/act/en/research/reports/act-publications/condition-of-college-and-career-readiness-2017.html

Creasy, J. A., Whipp, P. R., & Jackson, B. (2012). Teachers' pedagogical content knowledge and students' learning outcomes in ball game instruction. *ICHPER-SD Journal of Research, 7*(1), 3–11.

Crotty, J. (2014). If Massachusetts Were A Country, Its Students Would Rank 9th In The World. Retrieved November 24, 2020, from https://www.forbes.com/sites/jamesmarshallcrotty/2014/09/29/if-massachusetts-were-a-country-its-students-would-rank-9th-in-the-world/?sh=79a5c213149b

Dallimore, E. J., Hertenstein, J. H., & Platt, M. B. (2013). Impact of cold-calling on student *voluntary participation. Journal of Management Education, 37(3),* 305–341. https://doi.org/10.1177/1052562912446067

Damon, W. (2010). The path to purpose how young people find their calling in life. Free Press.

Davis, L. P., & Museus, S. D. (2019). Identifying and disrupting deficit thinking. Retrieved June 17, 2021, from https://medium.com/national-center-for-institutional-diversity/identifying-and-disrupting-deficit-thinking-cbc6da326995

Decker, D.M., D.P., & Christenson, S.L. (2007). Behaviorally at-risk African American students:The importance of student-teacher relationships for student outcomes. *Journal of School Psychology. 45(1), 83-109*

Delpit, L (1988). The Silenced dialogue: Power and pedagogy in educating other people's children. *Harvard Educational Review 58*:280–298. pp. 286, 296.

Delpit, L. (2006). *Other people's children: Cultural conflict in the classroom.* New York: New Press.

Dermol, V. (2017). Teaching Approaches to Encourage Entrepreneurial Mindset of Students. In *Management Challenges in a Network Economy: Proceedings of the MakeLearn and TIIM International Conference 2017* (pp. 651-656). ToKnowPress.

DiAngelo, R. J. (2020). *White fragility: Why it's so hard for white people to talk about racism.* Boston: Beacon Press.

Digest of Education Statistics, 2020. (2020, September). Retrieved June 16, 2021, from https://nces.ed.gov/programs/digest/d20/tables/dt20_211.60.asp?current.asp

Dolin, J., Black, P., Harlen, W., & Tiberghien, A. (2018). Exploring relations between formative and summative assessment. In *Transforming assessment* (pp. 53-80). Springer, Cham.

Douglas, B., Lewis, C. W., Douglas, A., Scott, M. E., & Garrison-Wade, D. (2008). The impact of white teachers on the academic achievement of black students: An exploratory qualitative analysis. *Educational Foundations, 22,* 47-62.

Dover, Alison G. (2013). Teaching for social justice: From conceptual frameworks to classroom practices. *Multicultural Perspectives (Mahwah, N.J.), 15*(1), 3-11.

Duncan, A. (2013). The Threat of Educational Stagnation and Complacency. Retrieved November 24, 2020, from https://www.ed.gov/news/ speeches/threat-educational-stagnation-and-complacency

Dunlosky J, Rawson KA, Marsh EJ, Nathan MJ, Willingham DT. Improving students' learning with effective learning techniques: Promising directions from cognitive and educational psychology. *Psychol Sci Public Interest. 2013 Jan;14(1):4-58. doi: 10.1177/1529100612453266. PMID: 26173288.*

Durlak, J. A., Weissberg, R. P., Dymnicki, A. B., Taylor, R. D. & Schellinger, K. B. (2011). The impact of enhancing students' social and emotional learning: A meta-analysis of school-based universal interventions. Child Development, 82: 405-432.

Dynarski, M. (2018). *Is The High School Graduation Rate Really Going Up?.* [online] Brookings. Available at: <https://www.brookings.edu/research/ is-the-high-school-graduation-rate-really-going-up/> [Accessed 27 November 2020].

Dweck, C. S. (2016). *Mindset: The new psychology of success. New York: Random House.*Education Expenditures by Country. (2020, May). Retrieved December 04, 2020, from https://nces.ed.gov/programs/ coe/indicator_cmd.asp

Education in China: A Snapshot (2016). O.E.C.D. https://www.oecd.org/china/ Education-in-China-a-snapshot.pdf

Ellis, G. W., Rudnitsky, A., & Silverstein, B. (2004). Using concept maps to enhance understanding in engineering education. *International Journal of Engineering Education, 20*(6), 1012-1021.

Ericsson, K. A., Krampe, R. T., & Tesch-Römer, C. (1993). The role of deliberate practice in the acquisition of expert performance. Psychological Review, 100(3), 363-406. doi:10.1037/0033-295x.100.3.363

Evans, C. M. (2020). Measuring student success skills: A review of the literature on collaboration. Dover, NH: National Center for the Improvement of Educational Assessment.

Evans, C. M. (2020). Measuring student success skills: A review of the literature on critical thinking. Dover, NH: National Center for the Improvement of Educational Assessment.

Executive Summary of the No Child Left Behind Act of 2001. (2007). Retrieved November 23, 2020, from https://www2.ed.gov/nclb/overview/intro/execsumm.html

Feniger, Yariv & Atia, Michael. (2019). Rethinking cause and effect: Analyzing economic growth and P.I.S.A. scores over a period of fifteen years.

Ferrance, E. (2000). *Action Research [Pamphlet]. Providence, RI: The Education Alliance.*

Fleckenstein, Johanna & Zimmermann, Friederike & Köller, Olaf & Möller, Jens. (2015). What Works in School? Expert and Novice Teachers' Beliefs about School Effectiveness. Frontline Learning Research. 3. 27-46. 10.14786/flr.v3i2.162.

Freeman, S., Eddy, S. L., McDonough, M., Smith, M. K., Okoroafor, N., Jordt, H., & Wenderoth, M. P. (2014). Active learning increases student performance in science, engineering, and mathematics. Proceedings of the national academy of sciences, 111(23), 8410-8415.

Freiberg, H. J. and Stein, T. A. (1999). "Measuring, improving and sustaining healthy learning envirnoments". In School Climate: Measuring, Improving and Sustaining Healthy Learning Environments. Edited by: Freiberg, H. J. 11Philadelphia, PA: Falmer Press.

Freire, P. (2018). *Pedagogy of the oppressed.* New York: Bloomsbury Academic.

Frey, W. (2019, July 17). Less than half of U.S. children under 15 are white, the census shows. Retrieved September 26, 2020, from https://www. brookings.edu/research/less-than-half-of-us-children-under-15-are-white-census-shows/

Fullan, M. (2007). *The new meaning of educational change* (4th ed.). New York: Teachers College Press.

Gaitan, C.D. (2012). Culture, literacy, and power in family–community–school–*relationships. Theory Into Practice, 51,* 305 - 311.

Garcia, E., & Weiss, E. (2017). *Education inequalities at the school starting gate (Rep.).* Retrieved June 13, 2021, from Economic Policy Institute website: https://files.epi.org/pdf/132500.pdf

Gay, G. (2002). Preparing for culturally responsive teaching. *Journal of teacher education, 53*(2), 106-116.

Gay, G. (2010). *Culturally responsive teaching: Theory, research, and practice.* New York: Teachers College Press, 31.

Good T.L., Wiley C.R.H., Florez I.R. (2009) Effective Teaching: an Emerging Synthesis. In: Saha L.J., Dworkin A.G. (eds) International Handbook of

Research on Teachers and Teaching. Springer International Handbooks of Education, vol 21. Springer, Boston, MA. https://doi.org/10.1007/978-0-387-73317-3_51

Graham, S., Kiuhara, S. A., & MacKay, M. (2020). The effects of writing on learning in science, social studies, and mathematics: A meta-analysis. Review of Educational Research, 90(2), 179-226.

Gudmundsdottir, S. (1987a). Learning to teach social studies: Case studies of Chris and Cathy. Paper presented at the Annual Meeting of the American Educational Research Association. Washington, D.C. (ERIC Document Reproduction Service NO. ED 290 700) Gudmundsdottir, S. (1987b). Pedagogical content knowledge: teachers' ways of knowing. Paper presented at the Annual Meeting of the American Educational Research Association.

Washington, D.C. (ERIC Document Reproduction Service NO. ED 290 701) Haberman, M. (1991). The pedagogy of poverty versus good teaching. Phi Delta Kappan, 73(4), 290-294

Hamilton, E. R., Rosenberg, J. M., & Akcaoglu, M. (2016). The substitution augmentation modification redefinition (SAMR) model: A critical review and suggestions for its use. TechTrends, 60(5), 433-441.

Hammond, Z. L. (2015). Culturally responsive teaching and the brain: Promoting authentic engagement and rigor among culturally and linguistically diverse students. Thousand Oaks, CA: Corwin Press.

Haney, W. (2000). The myth of the Texas miracle in education. Education Policy Analysis Archives, 8(41).

Hansen, M., Levesque, E., Valant, J., & Quintero, D. (2018). 2018 Brown Center Report on American Education: Trends in N.A.E.P. math, reading, and civics scores (Rep.). Retrieved November, 2020, from Brown Center on

Education Policy at Brooking website: 2018 Brown Center Report on American Education: Trends in N.A.E.P. math, reading, and civics scores

Hansen, M., & Quintero, D. (2021). Boosting teacher diversity requires bold, extensive action Focusing on Layoffs Alone Isn't Enough. Retrieved June 22, 2021, from https://www.brookings.edu/ blog/brown-center-chalkboard/2021/06/16/boosting-teacher-diversity-requires-boldextensiveaction/?utm_campaign=Brown+Center+on+Education+Policy&utm_medium=email&utm_content=135509654&utm_source=hs_email

Hansen, M., Valant, M., Harris, D., Bryk, A., Pecheone, K., Bassok, D., . . . West, N. (2016). Memos to the president on the future of education policy. Retrieved November 30, 2020, from https://www.brookings.edu/series/memos-to-the-president-on-the-future-of-education-policy/

Harris, D. N., Liu, L., & Li, R. (2020). *Is the Rise in High School Graduation Rates Real? High Stakes School Accountability and Strategic Behavior* (Rep.). Washington D.C. Streep, M.,

Hattie, J. (2010). Visible learning: A synthesis of over 800 meta-analyses relating to achievement. London: Routledge.

Henderson, A. T., Mapp, K. L., Johnson, V. R., & Davies, D. (2007). *Beyond the bake sale the essential guide to family-school partnerships*. New York, NY: The New Press.

Herold, B. (2016). 1-to-1 Laptop Initiatives Boost Student Scores, Study Finds. Retrieved May 28, 2021, from https://www.edweek.org/technology/1-to-1-laptop-initiatives-boost-student-scores-study-finds/2016/05

Highlights of U.S. P.I.S.A. 2018 Results Web Report (N.C.E.S. 2020-166). U.S. Department of Education. Institute of Education Sciences, National

Center for Education Statistics. Available at https://nces.ed.gov/ surveys/pisa/ pisa2018/index.asp

Hirsch, E. D. (1988). Cultural literacy: *What Every American Needs to Know*. New York, NY: Houghton Mifflin.

History and Innovation - What is the Nation's Report Card: N.A.E.P. (2020, October 7). Retrieved December 02, 2020, from https://nces.ed.gov/ nationsreportcard/about/timeline.aspx

Hoy, W. K. (2002). Faculty trust: A key to student achievement. *Journal of School Public Relations, 23*(2), 88-103.

Hunter, G. S. (2013). Out think how innovative leaders drive exceptional outcomes. San Francisco, CA: Jossey-Bass.

Immordino-Yang, Mary. (2016). Emotion, sociality, and the brains default mode network: Insights for educational practice and policy. *Policy Insights from the Behavioral and Brain Sciences. 3*. 10.1177/2372732216656869.

Jackson, C. K. (2018). What do test scores miss? The importance of teacher effects on non-test score outcomes. Journal of Political Economy, 126(5), 2072-2107.

James, W. (1890) The Principles of Psychology, Holt

Jason, Z. (2017). Bored Out of Their Minds. Harvard Graduate School of Education. https://www.gse.harvard.edu/news/ed/17/01/bored-out-their-minds.

Johnson, S. (2012). *Assessing learning in the primary classroom*. London: Routledge.

Johnson, A., & Elliott, S. (2020). Culturally relevant pedagogy: a model to guide cultural transformation in STEM departments. *Journal of Microbiology & Biology Education, 21(1), 05.*

Kaplan, L. S., & Owings, W. A. (2015). Introduction to the Principalship: Theory to Practice. New York, NY: Routledge.

Kautz, T., Heckman, J. J., Diris, R., Ter Weel, B., & Borghans, L. (2014). Fostering and measuring skills: Improving cognitive and non-cognitive skills to promote lifetime success (No. w20749). National Bureau of Economic Research.

Kelly, A. V. (2009). The curriculum: Theory and practice. Sage.

Kendi, I. X. (2021). How to be an antiracist. London: Vintage.

Kingston, S. (2018). Project based learning & student achievement: What does the research tell us? PBL Evidence Matters. 1(1), 1-11.

Klein, A. (2020). No Child Left Behind Overview: Definitions, Requirements, Criticisms, and More. Retrieved November 22, 2020, from https://www.edweek.org/ew/section/multimedia/no-child-left-behind-overview-definition-summary.html

Knowles, M. (1975) *Self-directed learning: A guide for learners and teachers, New York:* Cambridge Books.

Kooloos, J. G., Klaassen, T., Vereijken, M., Van Kuppeveld, S., Bolhuis, S., & Vorstenbosch, M. (2011). Collaborative group work: Effects of group size and assignment structure on learning gain, student satisfaction and perceived participation. Medical Teacher, 33(12), 983-988.

Kouakou, Konan Kan Elvis & Li, Cai & Akolgo, Isaac & Tchamekwen, Alida. (2019). Evolution view of Entrepreneurial Mindset Theory. *International Journal of Business and Social Science*. 10. 10.30845/ijbss.v10n6p13.

Kulik, C. -L. C., Kulik, J. A., & Bangert-Drowns, R. L. (1990). Effectiveness of mastery learning programs: A meta-analysis. Review of Educational Research, 60(2), 265-299.

Ladson-Billings, Gloria. "But That's Just Good Teaching! The Case for Culturally Relevant Pedagogy," Theory Into Practice, 34, no. 3 (1995): 476

Ladson-Billings, Gloria. (1994). The dreamkeepers: Successful teachers of black children (San Francisco, CA: Jossey-Bass, 1994);

Ladson-Billings, Gloria. (2006) "Yes, But How Do We Do It?' Practicing Culturally Relevant Pedagogy," in Julie Landsman and Chance W. Lewis, eds., White Teachers/Diverse Classrooms (Sterling, VA: Stylus Publishers, 2006): 162-177; and

Ladson-Billings, Gloria. (1995). Toward a theory of culturally relevant pedagogy. *American Educational Research Journal 32, no. 3*. 465-491,

Lee, V.E. & Smith, J.B. (1995) Effects of high-school restructuring and size on early gains in achievement and engagement, Sociology of Education, 68(4), 241-270.

Lewis, C.W., James, M., Hancock, S., & Hill-Jackson, V. (2008) Framing African American students' success and failure in urban settings. *Urban Education, 43*, 127-153

Lombardi, M. M. (2007). Authentic learning for the 21st century: An overview. *Educause learning initiative, 1*(2007), 1-12.

Luckett, Kathy, & Shay, Suellen. (2020). Reframing the curriculum: A transformative approach. Critical Studies in Education, 61(1), 50-65.

Marchese, T. J. (1987). Assessment update. Third down, ten years to go. AAHE bulletin, 40(4), 3-8.

Marzano, R. J. (2006). *Classroom assessment and grading that work.* *Association for* Supervision and Curriculum Development (ASCD).

Marzano, R. J. (2010). *Formative assesment & standard-based grading.* *Marzano Research Laboratory.*

Marzano, R., Pickering, D., & Heflebower, T. (2010). The highly engaged classroom: The classroom Strategies Series (Generating High Levels of Student Attention and Engagement). United States: Marzano Research.

Maslow, A. H. (1943). A theory of human motivation. Psychological Review, 50(4), 370-396. https://doi.org/10.1037/h0054346

Mellom, Paula J, Straubhaar, Rolf, Balderas, Carissa, Ariail, Michael, & Portes, Pedro R. (2018). "They come with nothing:" How professional development in a culturally responsive pedagogy shapes teacher attitudes towards Latino/a English language learners. Teaching and Teacher Education, 71, 98-107. https://doi.org/10.1016/j.tate.2017.12.013

Military expenditure (% of G.D.P.). (2019). Retrieved December 04, 2020, from https://data.worldbank.org/indicator/MS.MIL.XPND.GD.ZS

Milner, H.R. (2006). But good intentions are not enough: Theoretical and philosophical

relevance in teaching students of color. In J. Landsman & C. Lewis (Eds) *White teachers in diverse classrooms: A guide to building inclusive schools,*

promoting high expectations, and eliminating racism (pp. 79-90).
Sterling, VA: Stylus.

Misplaced Priorities: Over Incarcerate, Under Educate (Rep.). (2011, April). Retrieved June 13, 2021, from National Association for the Advancement of Colored People website: https://www.prisonpolicy.org/scans/naacp/misplaced_priorities.pdf

Monte-Sano, C., & Budano, C. (2013). Developing and enacting pedagogical content knowledge for teaching history: An exploration of two novice teachers' growth over three years. Journal of the Learning Sciences, 22(2), 171-211.

Moria, E., Refnaldi, R., & Zaim, M. (2017). Using authentic assessment to better facilitate teaching and learning: The case for students' writing assessment. In Sixth International Conference on Languages and Arts (ICLA 2017). Atlantis Press.

Murawski, W. W., & Scott, K. L. (Eds.). (2019). What really works with Universal Design forLearning. Corwin.

Murphy, V., Fox, J., Freeman, S., & Hughes, N. (2017). "Keeping it Real": A review of the benefits, challenges and steps towards implementing authentic assessment. All Ireland Journal of Higher Education, 9(3).

National Governors Association Center for Best Practices, Council of Chief State School Officers (2010) Common Core State Standards. National Governors Association Center for Best Practices, Council of Chief State School Officers, Washington D.C. Copyright Date: 2010. http://www.corestandards.org/

National Research Council. (2001). Educating Teachers of Science, Mathematics, and Technology: New Practices for the New Millennium.

Washington, DC: The National Academies Press. https://doi. org/10.17226/9832.

National School Climate Standards Benchmarks to promote effective teaching, learning and comprehensive school improvement. (2009). Retrieved February 01, 2021, from https://www.schoolclimate.org/

Nancekivell, S. E., Shaw, P., & Gelman, S. A. (2019). Maybe they're born with It, or maybe it's experience: Toward a deeper understanding of the learning style myth. Retrieved February 27, 2021, from https://www. apa.org/pubs/journals/releases/edu-edu0000366.pdf

Newmann, F., Marks, H., & Gamoran, A. (1996). Authentic pedagogy and student performance. *American Journal of Education, 104(4), 280-312. Retrieved June 8, 2021, from http://www.jstor.org/stable/1085433*

O.E.C.D. (2020), Reading performance (P.I.S.A.) (indicator). doi: 10.1787/79913c69-en(Accessed on November 23 2020)

O.E.C.D. (2020), Science performance (P.I.S.A.) (indicator). doi: 10.1787/91952204-en (Accessed on November 24 2020)

O.E.C.D. (2020), Mathematics performance (P.I.S.A.) (indicator). doi: 10.1787/04711c74-en (Accessed on November 24 2020)

Ohlson, M., Swanson, A., Adams-Manning, A., & Byrd, A. (2016). A culture of success-examining school culture and student outcomes via a performance framework. Journal of Education and Learning, 5(1), 114-127.

Ok, M. W., Rao, K., Bryant, B. R., & McDougall, D. (2017). Universal design for learning in pre-k to grade 12 classrooms: A systematic review of research. Exceptionality, 25(2), 116-138.

Organization for Economic Co-Operation and Development. (2008). (issue brief). Ten steps to equity in education. Retrieved from https://www.oecd.org/education/school/39989494.pdf

Patall, Erika & Cooper, Harris & Wynn, Susan. (2010). The effectiveness and relative importance of choice in the classroom. Journal of Educational Psychology. 102. 896-915. 10.1037/a0019545.

Pellegrino, J. W., & Hilton, M. L. (Eds.). (2013). Education for life and work: Developing transferable knowledge and skills in the 21st century. National Research Council. National Academies Press.

Popham, W. J. (2008). Classroom assessment: What teachers need to know (5th ed.). Boston: Pearson Education.

Popham, W.J. (2008). Transformative Assessment. Alexandria, VA: Association for Supervision and Curriculum Development

Powell, W., & Kusuma-Powell, O. (2011). How to teach now: Five keys to personalized learning in the global classroom. Alexandria, VA: ASCD.

Powell, W. W., & Snellman, K. (2004). The knowledge economy. Annu. Rev. Sociol., 30, 199-220.

Putnam, R. D. (2015). Our Kids: The American Dream in Crisis. New York, NY: Simon and Schuster.

Rafiola, R., Setyosari, P., Radjah, C., & Ramli, M. (2020). The effect of learning motivation, self-efficacy, and blended learning on students' achievement in the industrial revolution 4.0. International Journal of Emerging Technologies in Learning (iJET), 15(8), 71-82.

Reed, J., & Stoltz, P. G. (2011). Put your mindset to work. Penguin UK, London.

AN EDUCATION FOR THE 21ˢᵀ CENTURY:
A HANDBOOK FOR TEACHERS

Resnick, L.B., & Hall, M.W. (1998). Learning organizations for sustainable education reform. Daedalus, 127(4), 89-118

Roediger, H.L., III and Karpicke, J.D. (2006) The power of testing memory: basic research and implications for educational practice. Persp. Psychol. Sci. 1, 181–210

Romer, D., & Wolfers, J. (2011). Brookings papers on economic activity: Fall 2010. Washington, D.C.: Brookings Institution Press.

Rosenthal, R, and L. Jacobsen. Pygmalion in the classroom: teacher expectation and pupils' intellectual development. New York: Holt, Rinehart and Winston, 1968.

Rosenthal, R., and E. Y. Babad. 1985. Pygmalion in the gymnasium. Educational Leadership 43 (1): 36–39.

Saavedra, A.R., Liu Y., Haderlein, S.K., Rapaport, A., Garland, M., Hoepfner, D., Morgan, K.L., Hu, A., & Lucas Education Research. (2021). Project-based learning boosts student achievement in AP courses. Lucas Education Research.

Sanders, B. (2020). Council post: The power of social and emotional learning: Why SEL is more important than ever. Retrieved July 13, 2021, from https://www.forbes.com/sites/forbesnonprofitcouncil/2020/12/07/the-power-of-social-and-emotional-learning-why-sel-is-more-important-than-ever/?sh=6e9716507a29

Sanders, W. and Rivers, J. (1996). Cumulative and Residual Effects of Teachers on Future Student Academic Achievement. Knoxville, Tenn.: University of Tennessee Value-Added Research and Assessment Center.

Sarya, I W, Suarni, N K, Adnyana, I N B, & Suastra, I W. (2019). The effect of problem based learning and authentic assessment on students' natural science learning outcome by controlling achievement motivation. Journal of Physics. Conference Series, 1318(1), 12095. https://doi. org/10.1088/1742-6596/1318/1/012095

Scardamalia, M., & Bereiter, C. (1992). Text-based and knowledge based questioning by children. Cognition and instruction, 9(3), 177-199.

School Composition and the Black White Achievement Gap (Rep.). (2015, September 24). Retrieved September 25, 2020, from https://nces. ed.gov/nationsreportcard/subject/studies/pdf/school_composition_ and_the_bw_achievement_gap_2015.pdf

Schunk, D. H. (2012). Learning Theories an Educational Perspective sixth edition. Pearson.

Shabiralyani, G., Hasan, K. S., Hamad, N., & Iqbal, N. (2015). Impact of visual aids in enhancing the learning process case research: District Dera Ghazi Khan. Journal of education and practice, 6(19), 226-233.

Shulman, L.S. (1987). Knowledge and teaching: Foundations of the new reform. Harvard Educational Review (1987). 57, 1-22.

Shulman, L.S. (1986). Those who understand: Knowledge growth in teaching. Educational Researcher, 15(2), 4-14.

Simon Marginson (2019) Limitations of human capital theory, Studies in Higher Education, 44:2, 287-301, DOI: 10.1080/03075079.2017.1359823

Sklad, M., Diekstra, R., De Ritter, M., Ben, J., & Gravesteijn, C. (2012). Effectiveness of school-based universal social, emotional, and behavioral programs. Do they enhance students' development in the area of skill, behavior, and adjustment? Psychology and Schools, 49, 892- 909.

Sleeter, Christine E. (2012). Confronting the marginalization of culturally responsive pedagogy. *Urban Education (Beverly Hills, Calif.), 47(3), 562-584. https://doi.org/10.1177/0042085911431472*

Sloan, K., & Rockman, S. (201). History Day Works Findings from the National Program Evaluation (Rep.). Retrieved July 26, 2021, from National Hisgtory Day website: https://www.nhd.org/sites/default/files/ whynhdmatters/NHDReport_Final3.pdf

Stevens, K., Tracy, M., Baker, M., & Wolters, B. (2020). Still Left Behind How America' Schools Keep Failing Our Children (Rep.). American Enterprise Institute for Public Policy Research.

Squire LR, Genzel L, Wixted JT, Morris RG. (2015) Memory consolidation. Cold Spring Harb Perspect Biol. 7(8) doi: 10.1101/cshperspect.a021766

Swan, K., Grant, S. G., & Lee, J. (2019). Blueprinting an inquiry-based curriculum: Planning with the inquiry design model. Silver Spring, MD: National Council for the Social Studies.

Taie, S., & Westat, R. G. (2020). Characteristics of public and private elementary and secondary school teachers in the United States: Results from THE 2017-18 National Teacher and Principal SURVEY first look. Retrieved April 01, 2021, from https://nces.ed.gov/pubsearch/pubsinfo. asp?pubid=2020142REV

The Economic Impact of the Achievement Gap in America's Schools (Rep.). (2009, April). Retrieved June 13, 2021, from McKinsey & Company website: https://dropoutprevention.org/wp-content/uploads/2015/07/ ACHIEVEMENT_GAP_REPORT_20090512.pdf

Thomas, K. W. (2009). Intrinsic motivation at work: What really drives employee engagement. San Francisco: Berrett-Koehler.

Thompson, J. (2020). Measuring student success skills: A review of the literature on complex communication. Dover, NH: National Center for the Improvement of Educational Assessment.

Tucker, C. (2015). More than a Google search. Educational Leadership, 73(1), 78-79.
Tyack, D. B., Bernard, S. C., Mondale, S., & Patton, S. B. (2001). *School: The story of American   public education. Boston, MA: Beacon Press.*

Ujifusa, A. (2020, April 27). Standardized Testing Costs States $1.7 Billion a Year, Study Says. Retrieved December 03, 2020, from https://www.edweek.org/ew/articles/2012/11/29/13testcosts.h32.html

U.S. Census Bureau, (2019, October 02). Population Estimates Show Aging Across Race Groups Differs. Retrieved September 26, 2020, from https://www.census.gov/newsroom/press-releases/2019/estimates-characteristics.html

U.S. Department of Education. (1983). A Nation at Risk: The Imperative for Educational Reform. Washington D.C.: The National Commission on Excellence in Education https://www2.ed.gov/pubs/NatAtRisk/risk.html.

U.S. Department of Education. (2008). The Federal Role in Education. Retrieved November 18, 2020, from https://www2.ed.gov/about/overview/fed/role.html

U.S. Department of Education. (2010). An Overview of the U.S. Department of Education-- Pg 1.

U.S. Department of Education. https://www2.ed.gov/about/overview/focus/what.html

Wahba, M. A., & Bridwell, L. G. (1976). Maslow reconsidered: A review of research on the need hierarchy theory. Organizational Behavior and Human Performance, 15(2), 212-240. doi:10.1016/0030-5073(76)90038-6

Wagner, T. (2012). Creating innovators: The making of young people who will change the world. New York: Scribner.

Wagner, T. (2014). The global achievement gap: Why even our best schools don't teach the new survival skills our children need--and what we can do about it. New York, NY: Basic Books.

Washington, S. (2018, September 17). Diversity in schools must include curriculum. Retrieved July 11, 2021, from https://tcf.org/content/commentary/diversity-schools-must-include-   curriculum/?agreed=1

Watkins, C. (2005). Classrooms as learning communities: A review of research. London Review of Education, London review of education, 2005-03-01.

Watts, H. (1985). When teachers are researchers, teaching improves. Journal of Staff Development, 6 (2), 118-127.

Wiggins, Grant (1990) The case for authentic assessment. Practical Assessment, Research, and Evaluation: Vol. 2 , Article 2. DOI: https://doi.org/10.7275/ffb1-mm19

Wiggins, Grant. (1998). Ensuring authentic performance. Chapter 2 in Educative Assessment: Designing Assessments to Inform and Improve Student Performance. San Francisco: Jossey-Bass, pp. 21 – 42.

Wiggins, G., & Mctighe, J. (2005). Understanding by design, expanded 2Nd edition. Alexandria, VA: ASCD.

Willingham, Daniel. (2015) *Raising kids who read: What parents and teachers can do.* San Francisco: Jossey-Bass.

Wong, A. (2015, October 15). History class and the fictions about race in America. The Atlantic. Retrieved July 9, 2021, from History Class and the Fictions About Race in America

Wright, S. P., Horn, S. P., & Sanders, W. L. (1997). Teacher and classroom context effects on student achievement: Implications for teacher evaluation. *Journal of PersonnelEvaluation in Education, 11*, 57–67, p. 63.

Xerri, M. J., Radford, K., & Shacklock, K. (2018). Student engagement in academic activities: A social support perspective. Higher education, 75(4), 589-605.

Xinying, Z. (2014, May 14). School tests blamed for suicides. Retrieved November 26, 2020, from https://www.chinadaily.com.cn/china/2014-05/14/content_17505291.htm

Yair, G. (2000). Educational battlefields in America: The tug-of-war over students' engagement with instruction. *Sociology of education, 247-269.*

York, B. (2014). Know the Child: The Importance of Teacher Knowledge of Individual Students' Skills (KISS).

Zhao, Y. (2009). *Catching Up or Leading the Way: American Education in the Age of Globalism. Alexandria, VA: A.S.C.D.*

Made in the USA
Las Vegas, NV
20 January 2024

84551746R00108